CORONERS

Related titles from Law Society Publishing:

Conditional Fees (3rd edn)
Gordon Wignall

Civil Litigation Handbook (2nd edn)
General Editor: Suzanne Burn

Fatal Accidents
Clive Thomas

Fixed Fees in the Criminal Courts (2nd edn)
Anthony Edwards

Personal Injury Handbook
Nicholas Waller

Titles from Law Society Publishing can be ordered from all good bookshops or direct (telephone 0870 850 1422, email **lawsociety@prolog.uk.com** or visit our online shop at **www.lawsociety.org.uk/bookshop**).

CORONERS

A Guide to the New Law

David Urpeth

The Law Society

ISBN–13: 978–1–85328–833–3

Published in 2010 by the Law Society
113 Chancery Lane, London WC2A 1PL

Typeset by Columns Design Ltd, Reading
Printed by TJ International Ltd, Padstow, Cornwall

The paper used for the text pages of this book is FSC certified. FSC (the Forest Stewardship Council) is an international network to promote responsible management of the world's forests.

FSC
Mixed Sources
Product group from well-managed forests and other controlled sources

Cert no. SGS-COC-2482
www.fsc.org
© 1996 Forest Stewardship Council

CONTENTS

ABOUT THE AUTHOR

David Urpeth is a partner at national law firm Irwin Mitchell. He specialises in workplace injury cases and is Irwin Mitchell's national Head of Workplace Injuries.

David has civil proceedings higher rights of audience enabling him to represent clients in all civil courts.

He is a Personal Injury Panel member of the Law Society, member of the Association of Personal Injury Lawyers and a Fellow of the College of Personal Injury Law.

David is also a former President of the Sheffield and District Law Society. He has written and lectured widely on the subject of personal injury law. David is one of Her Majesty's Assistant Deputy Coroners.

PREFACE

Coroners have served society since 1194. The last major reform of the coroners jurisdiction was in 1887 (although there was some reform in 1926). Since then, here has been little national guidance and support. It is therefore not surprising that some critics have argued the coronial system is a postcode lottery.

Reform of the coronial system has long been overdue. The Government intends the current changes to address the weaknesses in the present coroner system, which were identified in the 2003 reports of the two major reviews which examined the service; the Fundamental Review of Death Certification and Investigation, under the chairmanship of Mr Tom Luce and the Shipman Enquiry, under Lady Justice Dame Janet Smith.

This publication is limited to the coronial aspects of the Coroners and Justice Act 2009, hereafter the 'Act'.

David Urpeth
January 2010

TABLE OF STATUTES

1 THE PASSAGE OF THE BILL THROUGH PARLIAMENT

1.1 OVERVIEW

This section provides a summary of the Bill's passage through parliament. It includes some of the concerns raised as to the content of the Bill and explains why the Act looks somewhat different from the Bill as originally presented.

The Coroners and Justice Bill was placed before parliament on 14 January 2009. At that time, Bridget Prentice MP, Parliamentary Under-Secretary of State for Justice stated that the provisions within the Bill focused on measures to:

- introduce a national coroner service for England and Wales, headed by a new Chief Coroner;
- improve the experience of those bereaved people coming into contact with the coroner system, giving them rights of appeal against coroners' decisions and setting out the general standards of service they can expect to receive;
- reduce delays and improve the quality and outcomes of investigations and inquests through improved powers and guidance for coroners, and the publication of statistics and reports to prevent deaths; and
- introduce a system – for deaths not investigated by the coroner – that enables independent scrutiny and confirmation of the medical cause of death in a way that is proportionate, consistent and transparent.

The Coroners and Death Certification Bill and the Law Reform, Victims and Witnesses Bill, announced in the draft legislative programme in May 2008, were combined, largely because they shared the same overriding aim – to provide a better service for members of the public when they come into contact with the coroner, death certification or justice systems in this country. The Government believed therefore that it made sense to address the reforms to these public services in the one Bill.

The key provisions of the Bill proposed the following:

- introduction of a Chief Coroner;
- introduction of a new death certification system;
- relaxation of rigid boundary restrictions (but services to remain based within local authorities);

- an appeals system;
- independent inspection;
- new coroner areas;
- new appointment system for coroners;
- powers to secure information and evidence;
- inquests, few and far between, to be held in private where non-publicly disclosable material is relevant to proceedings.

In addition to the Bill there was a proposed Charter for Bereaved People who come into contact with a reformed coroner system. The charter was intended to set out the services bereaved families could expect in a reformed coroner system, and what they could do if these standards were not met.

1.2 RESPONSE TO THE BILL

When announced, the Bill received qualified support from various quarters.

1.2.1 Coroners' Society of England and Wales

The Coroners' Society of England and Wales issued its initial observations on the day the Bill was introduced. The Society, which was founded in 1846, had the following objectives:

(a) the promotion of the usefulness of the office of coroner to the public;

(b) the ascertainment in questions of difficulty of the duties which devolve on coroners;

(c) the advancement of such amendments to the law as seem desirable;

(d) the establishment and maintenance of contact with HM Government; and

(e) the protection of the rights and interest of coroners.

Andre Rebello, the Honorary Secretary said:

> On behalf of the Society and its members, I broadly welcome the publication of the Coroners and Justice Bill. I believe this Bill has the potential to provide a solid foundation, upon which a modern coroners' service can be developed.

Mr Rebello added:

> The Bill has been long awaited and now it is here, the work starts. The Society will continue to assist the minister in enabling the policy to be translated into the reformed Coroner Service. The detail will be in the rules, regulations and Practice Directions.

1.2.2 APIL

The Association of Personal Injury Lawyers, APIL, issued a briefing note in which Russell Whiting, APIL's Parliamentary Officer said:

> The coroners system in England and Wales has been in need of reform for a considerable time. The current system is inefficient and chaotic, and bereaved families deserve an efficient, supportive and well funded coroners system … We commend the Government for bringing forward the Coroners and Justice Bill …

Mr Whiting added that:

> Bereaved families should have access to legal advice before inquests and legal representation during inquests.

His comments included a call for the relaxation of the rules surrounding the grant of public funding.

1.2.3 INQUEST

INQUEST (which was founded in 1981 following a number of controversial deaths in prison and in police custody) issued a briefing in February 2009 which ran to 32 pages. Helen Shaw and Deborah Coles, Co-Directors of INQUEST said:

> INQUEST is proud to be associated with the process that has led to this Bill finally being considered by parliament … However, we would wish to emphasise that there remains no room for complacency. The proposed legal instrument retains several defects of principle and practice in its current form which, if not eliminated or modified … cause significant concern.

INQUEST urged the Government to consider *inter alia*:

- the development of specialist areas of knowledge and complex cases being heard before specialist coroners;
- enshrining in the legislation a positive duty on death prevention;
- the clauses which affect the numbers of jurors and jury involvement; and
- proper provision for families to have representation at inquests.

1.2.4 General

The three organisations mentioned above are just examples of organisations commenting on the Bill within a month of it being first laid before parliament.

It was clear, even at this stage, that although the Bill was supported in broad terms, it was not going to have an easy journey through the legislative process. There were still many questions left unanswered, not least the issues surrounding funding. Indeed, even during its first committee stages, there was critical comment about coroners reform being part of a much larger Bill.

Mr Edward Garnier MP (Harborough) (Con.) said:

> Why has the legislative process not been managed in such a way that we have a discrete Coroners Bill? We were promised one a while ago. Would it not be more sensible to run the reform of the coroner system through a discrete Bill, rather than tagging matters relating to legal aid, vulnerable and intimidated witnesses, and other substantive criminal justice issues onto this Bill?

Critics would answer that death is not an important political issue. However, death comes sharply into focus when it involves your own loved one. At that point, bereavement care and the coroner's service can be hugely important.

1.3 PARLIAMENTARY QUESTIONS

1.3.1 Joint Committee on Human Rights

The Bill caused many to look at the possible human rights issues that would arise. Andrew Dismore MP, Chair, Joint Committee on Human Rights queried the compatibility of the Bill with the UK's human rights obligations and asked several questions (which are detailed underneath the relevant clauses) in a 16-page letter to Right Honourable Jack Straw, Secretary of State for Justice. The letter is instructive and the most pertinent parts are reproduced below.

> **LETTER TO RT HON JACK STRAW MP, SECRETARY OF STATE FOR JUSTICE, DATED 12 FEBRUARY 2009**
>
> The Joint Committee on Human Rights is currently scrutinising the Coroners and Justice Bill for compatibility with the United Kingdom's human rights obligations. This is a lengthy Bill covering a number of discrete areas and raising a number of significant human rights issues. It is one of the Committee's priorities for legislative scrutiny for this session.
>
> I would be grateful if you could provide me with some further information about the Government's views on compatibility.
>
> ...
>
> **Duty to investigate (Clause 1)**
>
> The Bill sets a statutory duty on senior coroners to investigate certain deaths. The Explanatory Notes explain the Government's view that this extension enhances the state's ability to meet its obligations under Article 2 ECHR in relation to a number of cases where the liberty of the subject may have been constrained, for example, in cases of persons who have died while being detained in a variety of contexts (such as, in prisons, by the police, in court cells, in young offender institutions, in secure training centres, in secure accommodation, under mental health or immigration and asylum legislation).
>
> 1. *Would the Government accept that the extension of the duty to investigate all deaths in mental health institutions, including deaths of patients who had voluntarily undertaken treatment, would be an human rights enhancing measure?*
>
> **Purpose of investigation and matters to be ascertained (Clause 5)**
>
> The Bill provides that the purpose of a coroner's investigation will be to ascertain who the deceased was, and how, when and where the deceased came by his or her death (Clause 5(1)). That provision is qualified to the extent that where 'necessary for the purpose of avoiding a breach of Convention rights (within the meaning of the Human Rights Act 1998), the purpose of an investigation includes ascertaining in what circumstances the deceased came by his or her death as contemplated by the House of Lords in *R* v. *HM Coroner ex p Middleton* [2004] 2 All ER 465 para.35 (Clause 5(2)).

There are cases where the scope of the procedural requirements of the Convention may not be clear, but where the public interest in protecting the right to life may justify a broader investigation into the circumstances of a death. These cases include circumstances where the Convention rights, guaranteed by the HRA, may or may not apply:

- death of a vulnerable person in a private care home;
- death in a private work place;
- death involving British state agents in circumstances where the HRA does not apply because of date of death (i.e. pre-HRA) or location of death (i.e. abroad);
- death abroad not involving British state agents but in circumstances where there is no prospect of adequate investigation by host state;
- deaths involving other circumstances which, if allowed to continue or recur, may result in the deaths of other members of the public.

That one of the primary functions of any effective coronial system should be to prevent the recurrence or continuation of circumstances creating a risk of death or to eliminate or reduce the risk of death created by such circumstances has, of course, been recognised elsewhere:

- Schedule 4 paragraph 6 of the Bill itself;
- the recommendations of the Report of a Fundamental Review 2003 (Cm 5831, Chapter 8, p.89);
- relevant domestic legal authority, including *R (on the application of Amin)* v. *Secretary of State for the Home Department* [2004] 1 AC 653 at para.31; *R (on the application of Takoushis)* v. *HM Coroner for Inner North London* [2006] 1 WLR 461, paras.39, 43 to 47; *Inner West London Coroner* v. *Channel 4 Television Corpn* [2008] 1 WLR 945, para.7 and 8); and
- section 4(7) of the Fatal Accidents and Sudden Death Inquiry (Scotland) Act 1976) which allows the investigating Sheriff in Scotland to determine, amongst other things, (a) where and when the death and any accident resulting in the death took place, (b) the cause or causes of the death and any such accident, (c) the reasonable precautions, if any, whereby the death and any accident resulting in the death might have been avoided, (d) the defects, if any, in any system of working which contributed to the death or any accident resulting in the death, and (e) any other facts which are relevant to the circumstances of the death.

2. *Does the Government accept that there may be cases where the HRA may not apply, or where the scope of the Convention may not be clear, but where the wider public interest in the right to life, the right to be free from inhuman and degrading treatment and the common law right to dignity might be served by a wider* Middleton-*type investigation into the circumstances of an individual death of the kind contemplated under Clause 5(2)?*

3. *In such cases, does the Government accept that a wider,* Middleton-*type investigation and inquest would provide an opportunity to learn valuable lessons, to prevent the occurrence or continuation of circumstances creating a risk of other deaths or to eliminate or reduce the risk of such deaths (and so, reduce the risk of future Article 2 ECHR violations)?*

4. *Accordingly, does the Government accept that the Coroner should have a residual discretion to undertake a* Middleton-*type investigation and inquest in circumstances where the public interest might be best served by doing so even if those circumstances are outside the strict ambit of Clause 5(2)?*

Juries (Clauses 7–9)

The Bill changes current provisions in respect of jury inquests in a number of ways:

- The existing requirement to summon a jury in cases where the death has occurred in prison is extended to cover cases where 'the deceased died in custody or otherwise in state detention' [1] or where 'the death resulted from an act or omission' of a police officer;

- The existing requirement to summon a jury in cases where the death 'occurred in circumstances the continuance or possible recurrence of which may be prejudicial to the health and safety of members of the public or a section of it' [2] is removed;
- However, a new wide residual discretion is introduced for Coroners to summon a jury if there is 'sufficient reason' to do so;
- It is proposed to reduce the number of members of an inquest jury from 7–11 to 6–9.

5. *Please explain why the Government considers that it is appropriate to remove the existing provision for compulsory jury inquests in cases where the health and safety of the public may be at risk, bearing in mind the Convention rights that will generally be engaged in such cases.*

6. *What additional circumstances would be required for a jury to be summoned (what would be a 'sufficient reason' for a jury inquest?) and would these circumstances include cases where a risk to the health and safety of the public was engaged and where a report from the coroner may be necessary to avoid future deaths?*

7. *Does the Government consider that public confidence in the outcome of the inquest, and in the process as a whole, will be diminished by a reduction in jury numbers from 7–11 to 6–9, particularly in cases where Convention rights are engaged, and if not, why not?*

Outcome of investigation (Clause 10)

The Bill enshrines in primary legislation the existing prohibition on any determination by a coroner or jury which is 'framed in such a way as to appear to determine any question of (a) criminal liability on the part of any named person or (b) civil liability'.

These words as they currently stand in secondary legislation [3] have been held on a number of occasions [4] to have a meaning such that they could not defeat the purpose of an inquest to determine 'how' the deceased came by his or her death.

A narrow reading of the prohibition in primary legislation could serve to prevent verdicts currently open to coroners and their juries such as 'unlawful killing' or 'death as a result of neglect' or, indeed, to obstruct compliance with Article 2 ECHR. The Convention requires that an investigation compliant with Article 2 ECHR must be capable of leading to the identification and punishment of those responsible for a death, including a determination as to the legality of any act or omission resulting in the death. The Explanatory Notes correctly recognise that this requirement concerns procedure rather than results. [5]

The relevant issue in an inquest is responsibility and not liability. The coroner or jury should be free to describe the acts or omissions which are responsible for a death, without any restriction by reference to whether or not such a description might 'appear' to determine liability.

8. *I would be grateful if you could confirm that these provisions are not intended to change the current position under the Coroners Rules, and where a finding which might point to responsibility for a death is required by the Convention, that finding would not be inconsistent with the proposals in Clause 10.*

9. *I would also be grateful if you could confirm that the Government intend verdicts such as 'unlawful killing' or 'death as a result of neglect' to remain open to coroners?*

10. *Do you accept that the exclusion of findings which 'appear to determine' civil or criminal liability could lead to some ambiguity and unnecessary caution on the part of a Coroner or a jury keen not to appear to determine liability?*

11. *Is there any reason why the exclusion in Clause 10 should not be limited to findings which determine any question of criminal or civil liability on the part of any named person or body, in order to avoid any such unnecessary ambiguity?*

Certified investigations (Clauses 11–13)

During public bill committee proceedings, the minister was asked to explain how many cases had been affected by the absence of the proposed 'certified' investigation procedure. It became clear that the minister considered that there had been two cases which had been affected. [6]

12. *I would be grateful if you could confirm (a) how many cases have been affected by the inability to disclose certain information (despite existing special measures, including the potential to apply for PII in respect of that information); and (b) how those cases have been affected.*

The committee expressed concerns that these earlier proposals would be incompatible with the obligations of the UK under Article 2 ECHR and proposed that they be reconsidered in the context of this bill. [7]

13. *What has happened since these proposals were withdrawn from the counter-terrorism bill during the last session, to persuade the Government that it is necessary to broaden the reasons for certification to include a protection for witnesses and a new 'public interest' category?*
    - *in what sorts of circumstances does the Government envisage issuing a certificate for these purposes? Can you give some hypothetical examples?*
    - *certification for the purposes of protecting a relationship with another country is very broad. In what circumstances would the Government envisage issuing a certificate for this purpose? For example, would the Government issue a certificate (a) to save embarrassment of UK allies in cases of friendly fire and/or (b) to protect a trade or other commercial relationship between a UK company and a third party government?*

The Explanatory Notes explain that Article 2 ECHR does not require, in the Government's view, involvement of the bereaved family in all circumstances:

Article 2 does not give the public and next-of-kin an absolute right to be present at all times or to see all the material relevant to the investigation. The Government considers that the courts are very likely to accept that it is consistent with Article 2 for sensitive material not to be made public or disclosed to the next-of-kin where this is required by a substantial public interest.

14. *I would be grateful if you could provide a more detailed explanation of the Government's view. In particular, please provide any legal authority for the Government's position that the proposals are likely to be compatible with Article 2 ECHR.*

There is no express provision on the face of the Bill for special advocates to be available to represent the interests of interested parties in a certified inquest; instead it is suggested that the responsibility of examining any sensitive material and testing it on behalf of the deceased's family or next of kin could be left to counsel to the inquest 'acting in effect as special advocate'. [8]

15. *I would be grateful if you could provide further reasons for the Government's view that counsel for an inquest will be able to perform the functions of a special advocate*

on behalf of the deceased's family or next of kin, bearing in mind that the primary duty of counsel to the inquest will be, by definition, to the coroner rather than any of the interested parties. Specifically:

- *in any case involving certification, will the coroner be required to appoint an individual with clearance to act as a special advocate?*
- *how will that individual reconcile his duty to the inquest and the interests of what may be a diverse range of interested parties?*

16. *If this is an important safeguard for the rights of interested parties, why should the requirement for the coroner to appoint a special advocate or multiple advocates in cases involving certification not be provided for on the face of the Bill?*

The Bill currently provides for the Secretary of State to issue a certificate, subject to judicial review of his opinion that certain information should not be made public.

17. *Does the Government accept that the Minister must have reasonable grounds to support his opinion (a) that the relevant information should not be made public; (b) that the relevant reasons are satisfied and (c) that other measures would not be adequate?*
18. *If so, why shouldn't the Bill should be amended to clearly reflect this requirement?*
19. *What would the Government do if judicial review led to a certificate being overturned? (Wouldn't this pose the same problem which the Secretary of State considers would be associated with an application for PII?)*
20. *Given the importance of judicial oversight, why shouldn't the Bill be amended to provide the Secretary of State with the power to certify that certain information should not be made public, but to leave the appropriate measures necessary to achieve this (including the potential for sitting in private and without a jury) to the discretion of the High Court judge hearing the certified inquest?*

Powers to gather evidence and to enter, search and seize relevant items (Clause 24, Schedule 4 Paras 1–5)

The Bill makes provision for enhanced investigatory powers for coroners, including in respect of powers to summon witnesses and compel the production of witnesses. It also makes new provision for enhanced powers of search and seizure.

21. *Does the Minister consider that these powers would enable a coroner to compel an individual to produce evidence which would open him or her to criminal liability? If not, I would be grateful if you could explain the Government's view. If so, please explain why there should not be a specific exemption on the face of the Bill to deal with this issue.*
22. *Will the Coroner be required to disclose evidence gathered using these compulsory powers to interested parties?*
23. *Does the power to require a person to produce documents include a power to require full and appropriate disclosure and inspection to be provided by each interested party to all other interested parties, reflecting a duty on the Coroner to ensure full and appropriate disclosure and inspection for all interested parties, including bereaved families? If so, why shouldn't this power and duty be reflected on the face of the Bill?*

We expressed some concern about the breadth of these powers when they were proposed in the draft Coroners Bill and suggested that similar safeguards to those in

Part II of the Police and Criminal Evidence Act 1984 (PACE 1984) should be provided on the face of the Bill.

The Explanatory Notes indicate that the Government may introduce further safeguards in secondary legislation, including for such coronial functions to be delegated and details of to whom search and seizure powers could be delegated. Additional safeguards could include the provision of a record of items seized and for the return of seized items. They will also provide for a mechanism of complaint, by aggrieved individuals, to the Chief Coroner.

24. *I would be grateful if you could explain why comparable safeguards to those in Part II, PACE 1984 should not be provided on the face of this Bill.*

25. *Has the Government produced any draft Regulations to accompany these powers? If so, I would be grateful if you could provide my Committee with a copy to assist our scrutiny of the Bill.*

Power to report if risk of future death (Clause 24, Schedule 4 Para 6)

This power has the potential to enhance the ability of the state to comply with its positive obligation to take appropriate steps to safeguard the lives of those within its jurisdiction (Article 2 ECHR). However, Schedule 4 does not provide a mechanism for ensuring that recommendations are made, recorded or disseminated. There are no sanctions proposed for failure to respond to a report when one is made.

26. *There are a number of actions which could enhance the effectiveness of the Coroner's Report, and so, enhance the protection for the right to life. I would be grateful if you could explain the reason the Government chose not to use the Bill to:*

    - *Impose a duty on the coroner to make a report if he considers that action is required;*
    - *Impose sanctions for failure to respond on the part of the authorities receiving the report;*
    - *Require disclosure of the report and response thereto to all interested persons, and publication where appropriate;*
    - *Create a mechanism for monitoring and scrutinising such reports and responses thereto in the interests of ensuring that lessons are learnt.*

Governance: Chief Coroner etc (Clauses 27–31, Schedules 7–8)

The Explanatory Notes explain that the Chief Coroner will introduce training requirements which would 'ensure that all those working within the service are aware of and apply best practice, relevant guidelines and standards … and other developments in legislation'. Nothing on the face of the Bill requires the Chief Coroner to establish training requirements, nor does the Bill require any training to include information on relevant guidelines or standards.

27. *Why shouldn't the Bill require the Chief Coroner to institute a system of mandatory national training requirements for coroners, including provision for training in respect of Convention rights and the requirements of the HRA 1998?*

The Bill provides that the Chief Coroner will hear appeals against certain decisions of coroners, subject to further appeal to the Court of Appeal on a point of law. [9] The Lord Chancellor will have discretion to add or remove appeal rights. [10]

28. *I would be grateful [if]you could clarify whether it is the Government's intention that a decision that can be the subject of appeal to the Chief Coroner may no longer*

be subject of challenge by judicial review? When an appeal to the Chief Coroner is not available, will it be open to an Interested Party to seek judicial review?

29. *In view of the importance of the role in the proposed new scheme and the nature of the powers that go with that role, including the power to determine appeals, does the Government agree that it would be appropriate for the Chief Coroner to be a High Court judge (rather than a circuit judge)?*

30. *I would be grateful why you could explain why the Government consider that it is appropriate to allow the Lord Chancellor to remove proposed appeal rights by secondary legislation.*

The Bill provides the Chief Coroner with the power to conduct and carry out any inquest, or to invite the Lord Chief Justice to nominate a High Court or a Circuit judge to do so, in cases where that may be appropriate by virtue of 'particularly complex legal characteristics'. [11]

31. *I would be grateful if you could provide further information about the breadth of this test. For example, would cases such as the investigation of the shooting of Jean Charles de Menezes or the inquiry into the death of the Princess of Wales, be covered by this power?*

32. *In high-profile cases engaging Convention rights, but not necessarily raising any new or complex legal characteristics, would the Chief Coroner still have the option to take over the conduct of an inquest or to ask for the appointment of a senior judge to hear it in the place of a senior coroner?*

Governance: Guidance, regulations and rules (Clauses 32–34)

33. *Does the Government intend to seek any substantive changes to existing Coroners Rules, other than those made on the face of the Bill? If so, will draft Regulations and Rules be provided for scrutiny during the passage of this Bill?*

34. *In the light of the nature of the positive duty of the state in arranging inquiries into deaths where the Convention obligations of the state may be engaged, I would be grateful if you could explain the role that the Lord Chancellor will play in the setting of practice and procedure rules. In addition, I would be grateful if you could set out the Government's view that this continuing involvement is appropriate.*

35. *I would be grateful if you could explain how coroners and practitioners will be involved in the setting of practice and procedure rules. Would it be appropriate to create a new Rules Committee, similar to the rules committees operating in relation to the Civil Procedure Rules?*

Legal Aid

In our correspondence with the Minister on the draft Coroners Bill, we highlighted the availability of legal aid for bereaved families as an important consideration for the purposes of facilitating their effective participation and ensuring compliance with Article 2 ECHR. Our predecessor Committee recommended that legal aid should be available for families in any case involving a death in custody. [12] During the second reading debate on the Bill, the Lord Chancellor explained that the Government would consider amendments to the Bill for the purpose of broadening access to legal aid for bereaved families. He made the following qualification, explaining the Government's views:

'The reason why successive Governments have resisted a general provision to make representation or legal aid available in inquests is that they are civil, inquisitorial inquiries. They are not judicial proceedings, and they work very differently even from other civil proceedings.' [13]

During the Public Bill Committee debates on the Bill, the Minister, Bridget Prentice MP, also indicated that the Government would consider again the provision of legal aid to assist bereaved families participating in inquests.

36. *I would be grateful if you could explain further the Government's view that the current provision for legal aid for families participating in inquests which engage Article 2 ECHR is adequate to meet the requirements of the Convention for effective participation by the family.*

37. *Is there any reason why this Bill should not be amended to make express provision for access to legal aid for family members of the deceased in any inquiry engaging Convention rights (i.e. any inquiry under Clause 5(2))? …*

…

NOTES

1 As defined in the Explanatory Notes to Clause 1, and subject to the conditions that there is reason to suspect that the death was 'violent or unnatural' or its cause is unknown.

2 Section 8(3)(d) of the Coroners Act 1988.

3 Rule 42 of the Coroners Rules 1984.

4 *R* v. *HM Coroner ex p Jamieson* [1995] QB 1.

5 EN, paragraph 797.

6 Q 136, PBC Deb, 3 Feb 2009.

7 Thirtieth Report of 2007-08, paragraphs 112-121.

8 EN para 804.

9 Clauses 30(2) & (8).

10 Clause 30(5).

11 Clause 31 and paragraph 281 of the Explanatory Notes.

12 Third Report of 2004–05, Deaths in Custody, paragraph 309.

13 HC Deb, 29 Jan 2009, Col 28.

…

1.4 THE COMMITTEE STAGE

1.4.1 Public Bill Committee

Oral evidence on the coroner and death certification provisions was taken by the Public Bill Committee on 3 and 5 February 2009. Witnesses included representatives of the Coroners' Society of England and Wales, INQUEST, Cardiac Risk in the Young and the Royal College of Pathologists. Bridget Prentice, the Minister for Coroner Reform, gave evidence to the committee on 3 February.

The committee then spent six days scrutinising individual clauses of the Bill. The coroner and death certification clauses were looked at on 10 and 24 February. The remaining sessions were held on 26 February, and 3, 5 and 10 March.

As with any Bill, there were some aspects that were well received by the Public Bill Committee, and others where the committee raised questions about the approach and content.

Many aspects of the Bill were welcomed. These include:

- the Government's aim of improving the service to bereaved families, including the introduction of a charter;
- requiring investigations of all deaths in any form of state detention, rather than just prison;
- introducing a national Chief Coroner to provide leadership to the coroner system;
- introducing flexibility across coroner jurisdictions so that unexpected backlogs or emergency situations can be tackled more effectively;
- retaining the 'inquisitorial' nature of inquests so that they continue to find facts rather than apportion blame – in other words, keeping the distinction between coroners' courts and the civil or criminal courts;
- introducing a new and more accessible appeal system involving the Chief Coroner, to replace the current system of judicial review or appeals to the High Court with the approval of the Attorney General;
- making it clear that non-invasive magnetic resonance imaging (MRI) scans are permissible to determine the cause of death as an alternative to invasive post-mortems in some circumstances; and
- introducing a nationwide team of independent medical examiners to scrutinise the causes of death reported on death certificates in cases not requiring a coroner's post-mortem or an inquest.

The committee expressed some concerns about a number of issues. These included:

- proposals to allow inquests involving highly sensitive matters to be held partly in private and without a jury;
- the role of juries generally and the sort of cases they can be summoned for;
- ensuring better resources for those coroner areas which are currently considered under-funded;
- how to attach more importance to coroner reports and recommendations so that future deaths can be prevented;
- improving the support available for bereaved people at coroners' courts and out of hours; and
- how to ensure the new medical examiners are properly independent and work closely with coroners.

A number of amendments were suggested to the coroner and death certification clauses. In many cases, those moving the amendments made it clear that they were doing so in order to gain a better understanding of the Government's policy.

There were some major concerns which were put to a vote (all of which were won by the Government). These were:

1. Clause 5 (matters to be established by an investigation). There was concern

that it might unduly restrict juries' findings and should also make more of the possibility of preventing future deaths.

2. Clause 11 (certified investigations involving highly sensitive matters). The committee felt that inquests should be as open as possible and with juries when required.
3. Clause 18 (medical examiners). Some members of the committee felt that the Chief Coroner should be involved in appointing the new medical examiners.

Having listened carefully to the committee and considered the points that it had raised, Bridget Prentice agreed to reconsider a number of areas. These included:

- inquests involving highly sensitive matters (Clauses 11–13);
- more description in the Bill about the public protection role of coroners (Schedule 4, paragraph 6);
- leadership arrangements for the new medical examiners (Clause 18);
- whether coroners should be eligible to apply for the new Deputy Chief Coroner posts (Clause 27 and Schedule 7).
- whether to amend or re-instate the treasure provisions contained in the draft Bill published in 2006 (Clause 20 and potential new clauses).

Any changes the Government decided to make would be dealt with during the remaining parliamentary stages of the Bill.

1.4.2 Joint Committee on Human Rights

On 20 March 2009, the Joint Committee on Human Rights issued a report. The committee considered that Clauses 11 to 13, which provided for the Secretary of State to certify certain inquests so that they can go ahead without a jury and without the participation of the bereaved family, should be dropped from the Bill.

The committee did not consider that the Government had made the case for this provision; it said the proposal was too broad; and that the safeguards against infringement of Article 2 of the European Convention were inadequate.

Whilst the committee welcomed the implementation of numerous detailed reforms of the coroner system, which it believed enhanced the protection and promotion of human rights, the committee raised a number of detailed points about the scope of the provisions, in particular the proposed reduction in the size of juries in inquests, and legal aid.

The committee did not believe there was a good argument to have such publicly important matters being dealt with by a jury of as few as six people. It was concerned that this low number could adversely affect the quality of the decisions reached by juries.

The committee expressed significant concern over the issue of legal aid. The committee's report said the following:

> We are concerned by the evidence which we have received on the difficulties faced by families who seek legal assistance and representation to support their effective

> participation in an inquest where their loved one has died. Article 2 ECHR does not require legal aid to be provided in all cases. However, Article 2 ECHR will require legal aid to be provided where it is necessary to ensure that next-of-kin participation is effective. This may include legal aid for representation throughout an inquest.
>
> Evidence appears to suggest that current legal aid rules are being applied in a way which fails to recognise when legal aid may play an integral role in supporting effective participation for many families and that, in many cases, families are faced with unrealistic choices based upon the current application of the means testing rules.
>
> We welcome the undertaking of the Secretary of State and the Minister to look again at these rules. We recommend that the Government make a concrete commitment to an independent review of the current system for assessing access to legal aid and other funding for bereaved families to access legal advice and assistance, preparation and representation at an inquest.
>
> We suggest the following new clause for inclusion in the Bill which would ensure that the Government commissioned such a review and reported its conclusions to Parliament:
>
> Review of access to legal aid in inquests
>
> To move the following clause:
>
> (1) The Secretary of State shall, within one year after the date on which this Act receives Royal Assent, lay before both Houses of Parliament a report on access to legal aid and other funding for bereaved families in relation to inquests.
>
> (2) The report under subsection (1) shall be prepared by a person appointed by the Secretary of State following consultation with
>
> (a) the Lord Chief Justice; and
>
> (b) such other persons as the Secretary of State shall consider appropriate to consult.

The Bill completed its journey through the House of Commons following Report Stage and third reading on 23 and 24 March 2009. It then moved to the House of Lords where it received its first reading on 25 March.

1.5 HOUSE OF LORDS

1.5.1 First reading

The first reading in the House of Lords took place on 25 March but the second reading debate, due on 27 April, was postponed because other parliamentary business took precedence. Critics were concerned that this implied that the Bill was being given lower priority than it should receive. A new date for the second reading was not set at the time of the adjournment.

1.5.2 Second reading

The following statement was made by Parliamentary Under-Secretary of State, Ministry of Justice (Lord Bach) at the start of the second reading in the House of Lords (18 May 2009):

My Lords, I will be the first to admit that this is a wide-ranging Bill, but I make no apology for that. The Ministry of Justice and its partner agencies face many challenges. There are, quite rightly, increasing demands for more effective, transparent and responsive public services, enhanced public protection, improved access to justice and a strengthening of rights and responsibilities. The Bill will contribute to each of these outcomes.

It will help criminal justice agencies to focus on the needs of victims and witnesses, particularly the most vulnerable. It will strengthen the protection of the public through changes to the law on pornographic images of children and the sentencing of terrorist offenders. It will provide a more accessible and responsive coroner service for bereaved families. It will also help safeguard the public's right to have their personal information protected and reinforce the responsibilities on data controllers to comply with the data protection principles.

These are all high aspirations, but there is no reason why we should not strive to fulfil them and this Bill will play a part in that endeavour.

I turn now to the detailed provisions in the Bill. Part 1 lays the foundation for a wide-ranging reform of the coroner and death certification systems. The Shipman inquiry and the fundamental review of coroners and death certification both advocated a radical overhaul of the current arrangements. Two changes are essential and are at the core of the provisions in Part 1. The first is to place the needs of bereaved families at the heart of the coroner service and the second is to restore public confidence in the protection afforded by the death certification process, so the Bill will introduce a number of key reforms of the coroner system.

Bereaved families will, for the first time, have a clear legal standing in the investigations process, with new rights of appeal against coroners' decisions. The *Charter for Bereaved People*, a draft of which has been published alongside the Bill, will set out clear national standards of service for those who come into contact with the reformed coroner system.

While maintaining a locally delivered and funded service, the Bill introduces for the first time national leadership through a Chief Coroner. The Chief Coroner will be responsible for setting national standards, including those for training, supporting local coroners and hearing appeals against coroners' decisions.

I want to give your Lordships notice of some government amendments that I intend to bring forward in Committee which will introduce a further element to this national structure.

Aside from their heavy responsibilities for the investigation of certain deaths, coroners retain one residual function dating back to their 12th century origins; namely, the investigation of treasure finds. Following the debates in the other place, we are persuaded of the case for establishing a national coroner for treasure so that in future local coroners can devote all their time to their core responsibilities. I hope this decision will be particularly welcomed by the noble Lord, Lord Redesdale, my noble friend Lord Howarth of Newport and other noble Lords who have played an important role in this field and by their colleagues on the All-Party Group on Archaeology.

The Bill will also remove archaic restrictions on the transfer of investigations between coroners' areas so that inquests may more readily be held closer to the family of the deceased. Our reforms of the death certification system will see the introduction of a uniform process that is applicable irrespective of whether a body is to be buried or cremated. Central to these reforms will be the introduction of medical

> examiners who will independently verify medical certificates of the cause of death and provide medical advice to local coroners.
>
> Finally in this part of the Bill are the provisions relating to the certification of coroners' investigations. We introduced these provisions to address a very real issue; namely, how to ensure that there is an Article 2 compliant investigation in those very exceptional and rare cases where there is highly sensitive material, such as intercept evidence, that cannot be made public. That problem remains. But, as my right honourable friend the Lord Chancellor announced on Friday, we have concluded that the provisions in Clauses 11 and 12 do not command sufficient support and should be withdrawn. Where it is not possible to proceed with an inquest under the current arrangements, the Government will instead consider establishing an inquiry under the Inquiries Act 2005 to ascertain the circumstances in which the deceased came by his or her death.

Clauses 11 and 12 provided controversy throughout the Bill's passage. On 15 May the following ministerial statement had been made by the Lord Chancellor and Secretary of State for Justice (Jack Straw):

> In some rare but very important cases there may be highly sensitive information directly relevant to the circumstances of the death but which cannot be made public in any way. To meet this problem the Coroners and Justice Bill contains provisions to dispense with a jury inquest in certain tightly defined circumstances. These provisions have greatly been improved during their Commons' scrutiny. Now the decisions as to whether to hold a non-jury inquest would be made within the criteria by a High Court judge, sitting as a coroner. The main provisions on this are in clause 11. By clause 12 the blanket ban on the admission of intercept evidence was modified for the purposes of these special inquests.
>
> The government felt these changes struck a fair and proportionate balance between the interests of bereaved families, the need to protect sensitive material and judicial oversight of the whole process.
>
> However, following further discussions in the House and with interested parties it is clear the provisions still do not command the necessary cross-party support and in these circumstances the government will table amendments to remove clauses 11 and 12 (and the equivalent Northern Ireland provisions) from the Bill.
>
> Where it is not possible to proceed with an inquest under the current arrangements, the government will consider establishing an inquiry under the Inquiries Act 2005 to ascertain the circumstances the deceased came by his or her death. Each case will be looked at on its own individual merits. As with the provisions in respect of the certification of coroners' investigations, we would expect to resort to such a procedure only in very exceptional and rare circumstances.

1.5.3 Committee stage

The committee stage in the House of Lords took place between 9 June and 21 July 2009.

In June, during the opening sessions of the committee stage in the House of Lords, a formal amendment to the Bill, which would have enabled all bereaved families to obtain legal aid for representation, was rejected by the Government on grounds of cost. Lord Bach, the minister in charge of the Bill, said that if there was a 'bottomless pit of money' he would like to extend legal aid to many.

A Coroner for Treasure is to be created through the Government amendments. He or she will be responsible for investigating all treasure or treasure trove finds in England and Wales, and local coroners will no longer have jurisdiction in this area. This will free up local coroners to deal with death investigations and also ensure that treasure cases are resolved more quickly.

The Coroner for Treasure will have powers similar to those of a senior coroner, allowing him or her to summon witnesses and direct them to produce an item for investigation, which would include the actual treasure find.

1.5.4 Report stage

The report stage in the House of Lords commenced on 21 October and finished on 29 October.

On 21 October, it emerged that plans for secret inquests, which Justice Secretary Jack Straw had said were being dropped, were to be pushed through the House of Commons. The latest scheme would give the Lord Chancellor the absolute discretion to order a secret inquiry rather than a public inquest.

According to the proposals, relatives of the deceased could even be banned from such proceedings. The Government argued that secrecy is needed in a small number of cases to protect national security and aid the fight against crime but critics say it could be a way for the authorities to avoid proper scrutiny of their behaviour and decisions.

The measure was defeated when it was considered in the House of Lords on 21 October, but the Government said it would be reintroduced when the Bill returned to the Commons.

Human rights group Liberty said the powers would stop bereaved families from finding out the truth about how a loved one died.

1.5.5 Third reading and final stages

The third reading of the Bill took place on 4 November and the Bill entered the 'ping pong' stage on 9 November with intercept evidence the only remaining parliamentary contentious issue.

In a last-minute debate on the Coroners and Justice Bill, campaigners urged Jack Straw to abandon plans for secret inquiries into high-profile deaths following a revolt by Labour MPs. The Government's majority slumped to just eight as 30 Labour MPs trooped into the lobbies to vote against the Government. Labour MP, Andrew Dismore, led the revolt, complaining that the plan to hold secret inquiries into controversial deaths was actually worse than the Government's original idea of secret inquests, which was dropped following protests earlier in the year. Mr Straw insisted that some high-profile inquests should be suspended indefinitely so that a secret inquiry could be held instead.

Mr Dismore complained:

> Given the way that the Bill is currently phrased, there will be secret inquiries at the behest of the executive. The executive will set the terms of reference, the minister will choose the judge and the minister or the judge can restrict attendance at the inquest. The minister or the judge can restrict the disclosure or publication of evidence or documents.

Liberty director Shami Chakrabarti urged the Government to rethink its plans following the close 274 to 266 vote on Mr Dismore's amendment. She declared:

> The British public has no taste for secret justice, particularly when the rights of grieving families are at stake.

Justice unions parliamentary group secretary John McDonnell MP said:

> In the light of last night's vote, the government must listen to the principled stand many have taken and climb down from its dogged insistence on pushing these provisions through Parliament.

Mr Straw claimed that there would be a number of safeguards in the plan to use the Inquiries Act, which in any case would only happen in 'exceptional circumstances'. He went on:

> Those who say they don't like this and don't like the idea of non-jury inquests, I say, 'I don't like the idea of non-jury inquests'. What I'm trying to do here is square an extraordinarily difficult circle and have not yet found any way of doing it except by a route similar to this.

After narrowly avoiding defeat on this issue, the Government will have been delighted when the Bill received Royal Assent on 12 November 2009.

1.6 ROYAL ASSENT

Indeed, following Royal Assent, the Ministry of Justice issued a statement saying that:

> ... the Act will deliver a more responsive and transparent justice system for victims, witnesses and the wider public, and place bereaved families at the heart of the coroner service.
>
> The Act introduces the first major reforms for over 100 years of the coroner system by creating a new framework for England and Wales, establishing more consistent inspection and quality standards, and incorporating new rights of appeal for bereaved families who are unhappy with a coroner's decision.
>
> The new service, with national leadership provided by a new Chief Coroner, will reduce delays and improve the quality of investigations and inquests through improved powers and guidance for coroners. To prevent backlogs for both military and non-military inquests, investigations can now be transferred from one coroner area to another; and there will be clear standards so that all bereaved families receive the level of service they are entitled to expect. Knowledge gained from every death investigation will be applied more effectively for the prevention of further avoidable death and injury.
>
> There is provision, carefully circumscribed, for the establishment of a judicial inquiry under the 2005 Inquiries Act to take the place of an inquest, where there is

> highly sensitive evidence (typically intercept) and it would not be possible to have an Article 2 compliant inquest. These provisions will be used in rare cases only.

Jack Straw said:

> Coming into contact with the coroners system can be a daunting and complicated experience, at a particularly traumatic time, for those who have lost loved ones. Accessing the right information and support at the right time can make a real difference in finding resolution.
>
> That is why we are setting out national guidelines to establish consistent levels of service – so that members of the public know what they can expect.
>
> The provisions set out in the Act will simplify and strengthen the process for death certification in England and Wales by introducing a unified system for both burials and cremations and by appointing medical examiners to provide an independent scrutiny of the cause of death. This new system will address weaknesses in the present arrangements identified by the Shipman Inquiry and ensure that cause of death is confirmed in a way that is proportionate, consistent and transparent with additional safeguards for bereaved families.

On the day of the Act receiving Royal Assent, The Coroners' Society of England and Wales said:

> The Coroners' Society of England and Wales welcomes the Coroners and Justice Act 2009, which received Royal Assent today, the 12th November 2009.
>
> This is an historic landmark in the 815 year history of the Office of Coroner in that it is the first substantial reform since 1887. The Victorian legislation has served our communities well over the past 122 years, however in recent years the law has fallen behind as a result of changes to society and other legislative progress.
>
> Now that the foundations of reform have been laid by Parliament, the Coroners' Society looks forward to working with officials, the senior judiciary and other stakeholders on the rules, regulations and structures needed to continue with our public service after the Act has been implemented.
>
> The Society looks forward working with the soon to be appointed Chief Coroner and his office and together will ensure that government properly resources the new responsibilities, structures and services to give effect to the Coroner law reform.

1.7 CONCLUSIONS

It is clear that the coronial system was in need of major reform. It is equally clear that those working within the coronial system have done their very best to make the old system work despite its obvious deficiencies.

It is sincerely hoped that the Coroners and Justice Act 2009, together with the Charter for Bereaved People (when implemented), will provide a new platform for enhancing the coronial service. It is the author's opinion that there is the will from those working within the coronial service to work hard to make the new legislation a success.

Critics' biggest concern appears to be over the issue of funding. They argue that it was clear from the outset that the Government did not want to tackle the issue of a fragmented coronial service and place the reformed service on a national basis. Despite there being a Chief Coroner under the new Act, the service is never going to be as unified as it would have been had the service been provided on a national basis. One can only speculate that the reason for avoiding producing a national service was cost. Critics are therefore concerned as to where the funding is going to come from. Who is going to make local authorities increase their funding in the coronial system? Without such increased funding, critics fail to see how the reformed service will meet the expectations, both of those coming into contact as well as of those working within the coronial service.

Although the Government has gone some way to addressing problems with the coronial service, critics are left with the feeling that a chance has been missed to provide the comprehensive overhaul that was required.

The success or failure of the reforms will in large part be down to the rules, regulations and the Charter for Bereaved People brought in to support the Act. The author therefore hopes that in addition to resources being available to fund the new service, sufficient time, energy and resource is spent drafting the rules, regulations and Charter for Bereaved People so that we can see an improved and viable service, fit for purpose in the 21st century.

2 COMMENTARY ON THE CORONERS AND JUSTICE ACT 2009

2.1 INTRODUCTION

Most of the sections pertaining to coronial law are dealt with in the Act in Part 1 and the Schedules. It should be remembered that the success or otherwise of this Act will, in large measure, be down to the rules and regulations brought in to supplement the Act.

The relevant provisions of the Act itself are set out in full at **Appendix 1**.

The terms for coronial posts have changed under the new Act. The following table sets out the name changes:

Old title	**New title**
N/A	Chief Coroner
Coroner	Senior Coroner
Deputy Coroner	Area Coroner
Assistant Deputy Coroner	Assistant Coroner

Within this text, so as not to cause confusion between the new titles of 'senior coroner' and 'Chief Coroner', reference to 'coroner' is to be read as 'senior coroner'. Senior coroner is defined by the Act as the coroner appointed by the local authority.

2.2 PART 1, CHAPTER 1: INVESTIGATIONS INTO DEATHS

2.2.1 Duty to investigate

Duty to investigate certain deaths (s.1)

Under s.1(1) a coroner who is made aware that the body of a deceased person is within that coroner's area, must as soon as practicable conduct an investigation into the person's death if subsection (2) applies.

Subsection (2) retains the requirement to conduct an investigation into a person's death if:

- the deceased dies a violent or unnatural death;
- the cause of death is unknown; or
- the deceased died whilst in custody or otherwise in state detention.

Subsection (4) provides that a coroner who has reason to believe that the death has occurred in or near his area in circumstances such that there should be an investigation and a duty to conduct an investigation does not arise because of the destruction, loss or absence of the body, may report the matter to the Chief Coroner.

Subsection (5) enables the Chief Coroner who receives a report under subsection (4) to direct a coroner to conduct an investigation into the death.

Subsection (7) enables a coroner to make whatever enquiries seem necessary in order to decide whether a duty under subsection (1) arises or whether a power under subsection (4) arises.

2.2.2 Investigation by other coroner

Request for other coroner to conduct investigation (s.2)

Section 2(1) enables a coroner under a duty to conduct an investigation to request another coroner from another area to conduct that investigation.

Under subsection (2) if a coroner agrees to conduct an investigation requested under subsection (1), he must conduct the investigation as soon as practicable.

Under subsection (5), a coroner must give to the Chief Coroner notice in writing of any request made by him under subsection (1) stating whether or not the other coroner has agreed to it.

Section 2 is a significant change in the law and one which should be welcomed as it is intended to ensure that delays in the system are reduced by ensuring work can be transferred across districts.

Historically, work could only be transferred into another area if the area was adjoining. This restriction has been removed.

However, problems are likely to arise regarding funding. As the coronial service is not centrally funded, but funded by the local authorities for each coroner area, the local authority for area B might not want to accept a transfer from area A.

Direction for other coroner to conduct investigation (s.3)

Section 3(1) enables the Chief Coroner to direct a coroner to conduct an investigation into a person's death even though, apart from the direction, a different coroner in a different area would be under a duty to conduct it.

Subsection (4) requires the Chief Coroner to give notice in writing of the direction under this section.

Whilst again, the section ought to enable inquests to be dealt with more speedily, there may be problems with funding for such transfers. This lack of clarity is likely to lead to problems and possibly delay, which may, of course, defeat the purpose of the section.

2.2.3 Discontinuance of investigations

Discontinuance where cause of death revealed by post-mortem examination (s.4)

Section 4(1) requires a coroner to discontinue an examination where the post-mortem reveals the cause of death before he has begun holding an inquest and he does not think it necessary to continue the investigation.

So for example, if a person dies and the cause of death is not known, the death will be reported to the coroner who will order a post-mortem. If the post-mortem shows the cause of death was some natural cardiac event, e.g. myocardial infarction, then the investigations can cease at that point.

However, s.4(1)(b) permits the coroner to continue with his investigation. This discretion goes much further than the old law. As a result, coroners are likely to find themselves receiving submissions from interested persons to continue with investigations.

Section 4(2) states that subsection (1) does not apply if the coroner has reason to suspect that the deceased died a violent or unnatural death or died while in custody or otherwise in state detention.

Under subsection (4), a coroner who discontinues an investigation into a death under this section must, if requested to do so in writing by an interested person, give to that person as soon as practicable a written explanation as to why the investigation was discontinued.

2.2.4 Purpose of investigation

Matters to be ascertained (s.5)

Under s.5(1) the purpose of an investigation under Part 1 of the Act into a person's death is to ascertain:

(a) who the deceased was;

(b) how, when and where the deceased came by his or her death;

(c) the particulars (if any) required by the 1953 Act [Births and Deaths Registration Act 1953] to be registered concerning the death.

Under subsection (2), to ensure that there is not a breach of Article 2 of the European Convention on Human Rights (as defined in the Human Rights Act 1998) the 'how' is to be read as including 'in what circumstances' in appropriate cases, e.g. prison deaths.

Section 5(3) states that neither the coroner conducting an investigation nor the jury (if there is one) may express any opinion on any other matter subject to paragraph 6 of Schedule 4, which deals with actions to prevent other deaths.

2.2.5 Inquests

Duty to hold inquest (s.6)

This section merely confirms that subject to s.4(3)(a) – discontinuance where post-mortem establishes a natural cause of death – the coroner must hold an inquest.

There is no discretion whether or not to hold an inquest.

Whether jury required (s.7)

Jury inquests are very much the exception to the norm. Indeed, s.7(1) states that an inquest must be held without a jury unless subsections (2) or (3) apply.

Section 7(2) requires a jury if:

- the death occurred in custody/detention and the death was violent or unnatural or the cause was unknown; or
- the death resulted from the act or omission of a police officer or member of the force in the exercise of their duty; or
- the death was caused by a notifiable accident, poisoning or disease.

Regarding the first requirement, the new rule modifies the old rule which required *all* deaths in custody/detention to have a jury. This included visitors which made little sense.

The old rule also included those in custody/detention who had died a natural death. The new Act removes such deaths from the scope of the Act. Some are concerned about this change and will be watching closely to ensure that prison deaths are only reported as natural in *appropriate* cases.

For example, the second requirement would include circumstances where a police car crashes, killing a pedestrian.

The third requirement relates to deaths which are 'notifiable'. This would typically be deaths requiring notification to the Health and Safety Executive or local authority, e.g. workplace accidents.

In addition to the circumstances where a jury *must* be called, s.7(3) retains the discretion for a coroner to hear any inquest with a jury if he believes there is sufficient reason to do so.

Assembling a jury (s.8)

Under s.8(1) the jury at an inquest (where there is a jury) is to consist of seven, eight, nine, ten or eleven persons.

Critics of the original Bill were concerned that matters of such extreme public importance could be decided by as few as six people. They feared that this could lead to poor jury decisions. On its passage through parliament, the jury numbers were increased to what are now contained in s.8(1).

Whilst eligibility for service is the same as for the Crown Court, High Court and county courts, the number of jurors is lower.

Under subsection (5), the coroner may put to a person summoned under s.8 any questions that appear to be necessary to establish whether or not that person is qualified to serve as a juror at an inquest.

Determination and findings by a jury (s.9)

Normally the findings of the jury must be unanimous. A determination or finding need not be unanimous if:

- only one or two of the jury do not agree on it; and
- the jury has deliberated for a period of time that the coroner thinks reasonable in view of the nature and complexity of the case.

The foreman in a split jury must state publicly how many agreed and how many did not.

Under subsection (3), if the members of the jury, or the number of members required, do not agree on a determination or finding, the coroner may discharge the jury and another one may be summoned in its place.

2.2.6 Outcome of investigation

Determinations and findings to be made (s.10)

Under s.10(1), after hearing the evidence, the coroner (or jury if there is one) must make determinations pursuant to s.5(1), namely who the deceased was, where and when he died and how (or in what circumstances) and, if particulars are required by the Births and Deaths Registration Act 1953 to be registered concerning the death, make a finding as to those particulars.

Subsection (2) states that determinations cannot apportion blame. That clearly means they cannot suggest criminal or civil liability of a named individual.

In some cases, the appropriate verdict might be unlawful killing. On the face of it, such a verdict would appear to breach subsection (2). However, such a verdict would be delivered without naming any individual.

2.2.7 Suspension

Duty or power to suspend or resume investigations (s.11)

Schedule 1 makes provision about suspension and resumption of investigations. See comments on Schedule 1 below.

2.2.8 Death of service personnel abroad

Investigation in Scotland (s.12)

Under this section, if, at the time of the death, a person was involved in active service either as a member of the Armed Forces or as a civilian subject to service discipline or accompanying persons subject to service law, then, if the Secretary of State thinks it is appropriate for the circumstances of the death to be investigated, the Chief Coroner may notify the Lord Advocate accordingly.

Investigation in England and Wales despite body been brought to Scotland (s.13)

Under s.13(1) the Chief Coroner may direct a coroner to conduct an investigation into a person's death if the deceased was a member of the Armed Forces or a civilian subject to service discipline or accompanying persons subject to service law and the Lord Advocate notifies the Chief Coroner that it may be appropriate for an investigation to be conducted and the Chief Coroner has reason to suspect that:

- the deceased died a violent or unnatural death;
- the cause of death is unknown; or
- the deceased died while in custody or otherwise in state detention.

2.2.9 Ancillary powers of coroners in relation to deaths

Post-mortem examinations (s.14)

Section 14(1) enables a coroner to request a suitable practitioner to make a post-mortem examination of the body if:

> (a) the coroner is responsible for conducting an investigation under this Part into the death of the person in question, or
>
> (b) a post-mortem examination is necessary to enable the coroner to decide whether the death is one into which the coroner has a duty under section 1(1) to conduct an investigation.

Section 14(1)(b) is to deal with situations where it is unclear whether the death is natural or not and a post-mortem is required to establish this and therefore whether the coroner has a duty to investigate.

Subsection (4) puts into statute the common sense position that if the death was caused wholly or partly by the improper or negligent treatment of a registered medical practitioner or other person, that practitioner or other person must not make or assist in an examination of the body but is entitled to be represented at such an examination.

Under subsection (5), the person who makes a post-mortem examination must as soon as practicable report the results of the examination to the coroner.

Power to remove body (s.15)

Section 15(1) empowers the coroner to order the body to be removed to a suitable place for the purpose of conducting an investigation or post-mortem.

Subsection (2) confirms that place may be within the coroner's area or elsewhere.

Under subsection (3), the coroner may not order the removal of a body under this section to a place provided by a person who has not consented to its being removed there.

The purpose of s.15 is to enable transfer of bodies outside the normal jurisdictional area to ensure that investigations and inquests are conducted speedily.

2.2.10 Miscellaneous

Investigations lasting more than a year (s.16)

Under s.16(1), a coroner who is conducting an investigation into a person's death that has not been completed or discontinued within a year must notify the Chief Coroner of that fact and must also notify the Chief Coroner of the date on which the investigation is completed or discontinued.

The Chief Coroner must keep a register of such notifications.

Monitoring of and training for investigations into deaths of service personnel (s.17)

Under s.17(1), the Chief Coroner must monitor investigations into service deaths and ensure that coroners conducting such investigations are suitably trained to do so.

2.3 PART 1, CHAPTER 2: NOTIFICATION, CERTIFICATION AND REGISTRATION OF DEATHS

2.3.1 Notification by medical practitioner to senior coroner (s.18)

This section enables the Lord Chancellor to make regulations requiring a registered medical practitioner, in prescribed cases or circumstances, to notify the coroner of a death of which the practitioner is aware.

However, before making regulations under this section, the Lord Chancellor must consult the Secretary of State for Health and the Chief Coroner.

2.3.2 Medical examiners (s.19)

This section of the Act which creates the medical examiner is intended to improve the system of reporting and certification of deaths, the defects of which were noted in the reports mentioned in the **Preface** of this book.

Section 19(1) requires Primary Care Trusts (in England) and Local Health Boards (in Wales) to appoint persons as medical examiners to discharge the functions conferred on medical examiners under this Act.

Under subsection (2) each Trust or Board must appoint enough medical examiners and make available enough funds and other resources to enable those functions to be discharged in its area and to monitor the performance of medical examiners.

It is likely that the vast majority of medical examiners will fulfil their role on a part-time basis. There are two potential problems with this:

1. Although coroners themselves are available 24 hours a day, the coroner may find that they do not have access to a medical examiner at certain times of the day.
2. If several medical examiners are sharing the responsibility for a certain area, there may be problems with communication and continuity.

Subsection (3) states that a person may be appointed as a medical examiner only if, at the time of appointment, he or she:

- is a registered medical practitioner and has been throughout the previous five years; and
- practises as such or has done within the previous five years.

Under subsection (4), the appropriate Minister may by regulations make provision:

- about the terms of appointment and termination of appointment of medical examiners;
- for the payment to medical examiners;
- as to training;
- about the procedures to be followed in connection with the exercise of functions by medical examiners;
- conferring functions on medical examiners; or
- for functions of medical examiners to be exercised during a period of emergency by persons not meeting the normal criteria.

The last of the provisions mentioned above is intended to deal with exceptional circumstances, for example, a disaster, natural or otherwise.

These provisions in reality set out the terms of reference for medical examiners.

2.3.3 Medical certificate of cause of death (s.20)

Many people erroneously believe the medical certificate of cause of death (MCCD) is the death certificate. This is not the case. Only the Registrar of Births and Deaths can issue a death certificate and the MCCD occurs at a much earlier stage in the procedure.

Under s.20(1), the Secretary of State may, in relation to a death that is required to be registered under Part 2 of the Births and Deaths Registration Act 1953, make provision:

(a) requiring a registered medical practitioner who attended the deceased before his or her death to prepare the MCCD or, where he is unable to establish the cause of death, refer the case to the coroner;
(b) requiring a copy of an attending practitioner's certificate to be given to a medical examiner;
(c) allowing an attending practitioner, if invited to do so by the medical examiner or a registrar, to issue a fresh attending practitioner's certificate superseding the existing one;
(d) requiring a coroner to refer the case to a medical examiner;
(e) requiring a medical examiner to make whatever inquiries appear necessary in order to confirm or establish the cause of death;
(f) requiring a medical examiner to whom a copy of an attending practitioner's certificate has been given to confirm the cause of death stated on certificate or to refer the case to a coroner;
(g) for an attending practitioner's certificate, once cause of death has been confirmed, to be given to a registrar;
(h) requiring a medical examiner to whom a case has been referred by a coroner to issue a certificate stating the cause of death or, where the examiner is unable to establish the cause of death, to refer the case back to the coroner;
(i) for a medical examiner's certificate to be given to a registrar;
(j) allowing a medical examiner, if invited by the registrar, to issue a fresh medical examiner's certificate superseding the existing one;
(k) requiring a medical examiner or someone acting on his behalf to discuss the cause of death with the informant and give him or her the opportunity to mention any matter that might cause a coroner to think that the death should be investigated;
(l) for confirmation to be given in writing that the requirement referred to in paragraph (k) above has been complied with;
(m) prescribing forms for use by persons exercising functions under the regulations;
(n) requiring the Chief Medical Officer of the Department of Health to issue guidance, after consultation, as to how certificates or other forms are to be completed;
(o) for certificates or other forms under the regulations to be signed or otherwise authenticated.

2.3.4 National Medical Examiner (s.21)

Section 21(1) enables the Secretary of State to appoint a person as National Medical Examiner.

The National Medical Examiner is to have the function of issuing guidance to medical examiners and to carry out any other functions conferred by regulations made by the Secretary of State.

Under subsection (4), a person may only be appointed as the National Medical Examiner if at the time of the appointment he or she is a registered medical practitioner and has been for five years and practises as such or has done within the previous five years.

Under subsection (5), the appointment of the National Medical Examiner is to be on whatever terms and conditions the Secretary of State thinks appropriate.

2.4 PART 1, CHAPTER 3: CORONER AREAS, APPOINTMENTS ETC.

2.4.1 Coroner areas (s.22)

Schedule 2 makes provision about coroner areas. Many have argued the fact that the coronial system is still to be divided into separate areas will lead to inconsistency and the alleged continuation of a postcode lottery.

Indeed, in a briefing paper from Charles Smith of the British Lung Foundation (BLF) entitled, 'Improving coroners inquiries that follow a death from mesothelioma' the BLF said:

> Despite the creation of a national framework for the coroners system it will remain in essence a collection of local institutions. Adherence to national standards from local coroners cannot be taken for granted.

2.4.2 Appointment, etc. of senior coroners, area coroners and assistant coroners (s.23)

Schedule 3 makes provision about these appointments.

2.4.3 Provision of staff and accommodation (s.24)

Section 24(1) requires the relevant authority for a coroner area to ensure provision of staff and accommodation needed by the coroner for that area. The relevant authority must take into account the views of the coroner for that area. Subsection (1) only applies to staff other than those provided by the police authority.

Unfortunately, given that the funding of the coronial system is still going to be provided by each local authority, there is still likely to be somewhat of a postcode lottery both for those working within the system and more importantly for the bereaved.

2.5 PART 1, CHAPTER 4: INVESTIGATIONS CONCERNING TREASURE

2.5.1 Coroner for Treasure and Assistant Coroners for Treasure (s.25)

Many people are unaware that under the old law, coroners had an involvement when treasure was discovered. Given that many coroners did not have experience of dealing with treasure, it was argued that treasure finds should be handled by coroners with experience of this area. This argument was accepted.

As a result, Schedule 4 makes provision about the appointment of the Coroner for Treasure and Assistant Coroners for Treasure.

2.5.2 Investigations concerning treasure (s.26)

Section 26(1) requires that the Coroner for Treasure conducts an investigation concerning an object if he receives notification of the object under Treasure Act 1996, s.8(1) and the object is found within the coroner's area.

Subsection (2) gives discretion to conduct an investigation even where notification has not been given if the Coroner for Treasure has reason to suspect that the object is treasure or treasure trove and again is within the coroner's area.

The purpose of an investigation under s.26 is to ascertain whether or not the object in question is treasure or treasure trove and if so, who found it, where it was found and when it was found.

2.5.3 Inquests concerning treasure (s.27)

The Coroner for Treasure may hold an inquest concerning the object in question. The inquest must be held without a jury unless the Coroner for Treasure thinks there is sufficient reason for it to be held with a jury.

2.5.4 Outcome of investigations concerning treasure (s.28)

Where the Coroner for Treasure has conducted an investigation a determination in relation to the object must be made by the Coroner for Treasure after considering the evidence (where an inquest is not held), after hearing the evidence (where an inquest is held without a jury) or by the jury after hearing the evidence (where an inquest is held with a jury).

2.5.5 Exception to duty to investigate (s.29)

Under s.29(1), where the Coroner for Treasure is conducting, or proposes to conduct, an investigation concerning an object that would vest in the Crown under the Treasure Act 1996 or an object that would belong to the Crown under the law relating to treasure trove if the object was in fact treasure trove, the Secretary of State may give notice to the Coroner for Treasure disclaiming, on behalf of the Crown, any title that the Crown may have to the object.

Under subsection (2), where the Coroner for Treasure conducts, or proposes to conduct, an investigation concerning an object that would invest in the franchisee under the Treasure Act 1996 or an object that would belong to the franchisee under the law relating to treasure trove, the franchisee may give notice to the Coroner for Treasure disclaiming any title that the franchisee may have to the object.

A notice under subsection (1) or (2) may be given only before the making of a determination under s.28.

2.5.6 Duty to notify Coroner for Treasure etc. of acquisition of certain objects (s.30)

Section 30(1) deals with an amendment to the Treasure Act 1996 dealing with the duty to notify the coroner of acquisition of certain objects. The new s.8A requires a person who acquires property believing or having reasonable grounds to believe that it may be treasure to notify the Coroner for Treasure within 14 days.

Failure to do so renders the person guilty of an offence and under Treasure Act 1996, s.4 liable to imprisonment for a term not exceeding 51 weeks or a fine not exceeding level 5 on the standard scale or both.

2.5.7 Code of practice under the Treasure Act 1996 (s.31)

A code of practice under Treasure Act 1996, s.11 may make provision to do with objects in respect of which notice is given under Coroners and Justice Act 2009, s.29(1) or (2).

No civil liability on the part of the Coroner for Treasure arises where he or she delivers an object, or takes any other action, in accordance with the code of practice under Treasure Act 1996, s.11.

2.6 PART 1, CHAPTER 5: FURTHER PROVISION TO DO WITH INVESTIGATIONS AND DEATHS

2.6.1 Powers of coroners (s.32)

Schedule 5 deals with the powers of coroners and Coroners for Treasure.

2.6.2 Offences (s.33)

Schedule 6 makes provision about offences relating to jurors, witnesses and evidence.

2.6.3 Allowances, fees and expenses (s.34)

Schedule 7 makes provision about allowances, fees and expenses.

2.7 PART 1, CHAPTER 6: GOVERNANCE ETC.

2.7.1 Chief Coroner and Deputy Chief Coroners (s.35)

Schedule 8 makes provision about the appointment of the Chief Coroner and Deputy Chief Coroners.

Many had argued against the requirement for the Chief Coroner to be a High Court judge on the basis that this excludes from the post the many very experienced coroners within the system. Critics have observed that very few High Court judges, save for those within the family division, have experience of an inquisitorial system. As a result, s.35 and Schedule 8 were modified from the original Bill.

Under the Act, to be eligible for appointment as the Chief Coroner, a person must be a judge of the High Court or a circuit judge. To be a Deputy Chief Coroner, the person must be a judge of the High Court, a circuit judge, the Coroner for Treasure or a coroner. For both posts, the person must be under the age of 70.

2.7.2 Reports and advice to the Lord Chancellor from the Chief Coroner (s.36)

Under s.36(1), the Chief Coroner must give the Lord Chancellor a report for each calendar year.

The report must cover matters that the Chief Coroner wishes to bring to the attention of the Lord Chancellor and matters the Lord Chancellor has asked the Chief Coroner to cover in the report.

Under subsection (3), the report must contain an assessment for the year of the consistency of standards between coroner areas. It is likely that subsection (3) was inserted owing to concerns raised that the new system was unlikely to deal with problems of consistency across coronial areas.

The report must also contain a summary for the year of the number, nature and outcome of appeals and the matters reported under paragraphs 4 and 7 of Schedule 5 and the responses thereto.

2.7.3 Regulations about training (s.37)

The Chief Coroner, with the agreement of the Lord Chancellor, may make regulations about the training of coroners including the kind of training to be undertaken, the amount of training and the frequency with which it is undertaken.

This section goes some way to ensuring consistency in service delivery.

2.7.4 Medical Adviser and Deputy Medical Advisers to the Chief Coroner (s.38)

Schedule 9 makes provision about the appointment of the Medical Adviser to the Chief Coroner and Deputy Medical Advisers to the Chief Coroner.

2.7.5 Inspection of coroner system (s.39)

Section 39(1) imposes a duty on inspectors of court administration to inspect and report to the Lord Chancellor on the operation of the coroner system. This subsection does not enable inspectors to inspect persons making judicial decisions or exercising any judicial discretion nor to inspect the Chief Coroner or Deputy Chief Coroner carrying out any functions as such.

The idea of this section is to monitor the running of the coronial system throughout each area in an attempt to provide a level of consistency and ensure standards are maintained.

Under subsection (8), if a report recommends the taking of any action by a coroner or the Coroner for Treasure, the Lord Chancellor may give a direction requiring the coroner to take the action within a period specified in the direction.

2.7.6 Appeals to the Chief Coroner (s.40)

Prior to the inception of this Act, the only method of 'appeal' was judicial review which was time-consuming, complex and expensive. This section of the Act has therefore been welcomed by users of the coronial system.

Subsection (1) entitles an interested person to appeal to the Chief Coroner against any decision made by a coroner that falls within subsection (2).

Subsection (2) states that relevant decisions are:

(a) whether to conduct an investigation under Part 1 into a person's death;
(b) whether to discontinue an investigation under s.4;
(c) whether to resume, under Part 2 of Schedule 1, an investigation suspended under Part 1 of that Schedule;
(d) not to request a post-mortem examination under s.14;
(e) to request a post-mortem examination under that section of a body that has already been the subject of a post-mortem examination, unless the decision is to request an examination of a different kind from the one already carried out;
(f) to give a notice under paragraph 1 of Schedule 5;
(g) whether there should be a jury at an inquest;
(h) whether to exercise a power conferred by virtue of s.45(3)(a) to exclude persons from all or part of an inquest;
(i) those embodied in a determination as to the questions mentioned in s.5(1)(a) and (b) (read with s.5(2) where applicable);
(j) those embodied in a finding as to the particulars required by the Births and Deaths Registration Act 1953 to be registered concerning a death.

Under subsection (3), an interested person may appeal to the Chief Coroner against a decision made by the Coroner for Treasure (or an Assistant Coroner for Treasure) in connection with an object that is or may be treasure or treasure trove or an investigation or inquest under Part 1, Chapter 4 concerning such an object.

Subsection (4) states that an interested person may appeal to the Chief Coroner against a failure to make a decision that falls within subsection (2) or a decision of the kind mentioned in subsection (3).

Subsection (5) enables a person who the coroner decides is not an interested person to appeal to the Chief Coroner.

Under subsection (7), when considering the appeal, the Chief Coroner may consider all relevant evidence including evidence that concerns a matter arising after the date of the decision, determination or finding.

Under subsection (8) if the appeal is allowed, the Chief Coroner may do one or more of following:

(a) in the case of an appeal against a decision embodied in a determination or finding, amend the determination or finding or quash the determination or finding and order a fresh investigation;
(b) in the case of an appeal against a decision not embodied in a determination or finding, substitute any other decision that could have been made or quash the decision and remit the matter for a fresh decision;
(c) in the case of an appeal against a failure to make a decision, make any decision that could have been made or remit the matter for a decision to be made;
(d) make any order (including an order as to costs) that the Chief Coroner thinks appropriate.

Under subsection (9), a party to an appeal under this section may appeal on a question of law to the Court of Appeal.

Under subsection (10), the Court of Appeal may affirm the decision, substitute for the decision any decision that the Chief Coroner could have made or quash the decision and remit the matter to the Chief Coroner for a fresh decision.

In light of the provisions of this section, it is envisaged that there will be more appeals under the Act than previously. Many fear that this may add additional delay and expense to the coronial system.

2.7.7 Investigation by Chief Coroner or Coroner for Treasure or by judge, former judge or former coroner (s.41)

Schedule 10 makes provision for an investigation into a person's death to be carried out by the Chief Coroner or the Coroner for Treasure or by a judge, former judge or former coroner.

2.7.8 Guidance by the Lord Chancellor (s.42)

Section 42(1) enables the Lord Chancellor to issue guidance about the way in which the coroner system is expected to operate in relation to interested persons.

Subsection (2) states that guidance issued under this section may include provision:

(a) about the way in which such persons are able to participate in investigations under this Part into deaths;
(b) about the rights of such persons to appeal under s.40;

(c) about the role of coroners' officers and other staff in helping such persons to participate in investigations and to exercise rights of appeal.

2.8 PART 1, CHAPTER 7: SUPPLEMENTARY

2.8.1 Regulations and rules

Whilst the regulations and rules are mentioned in the latter part of the Act, their importance should not be underestimated. The effectiveness or otherwise of the Act will largely depend upon the regulations and rules implemented under the following three sections.

Coroners regulations (s.43)

Section 43(1) enables the Lord Chancellor to make regulations for regulating the practice and procedure in connection with investigations under Part 1, for regulating the practice and procedure at or in connection with examinations under s.14 and for regulating the practice and procedure at or in connection with exhumations.

Subsection (3) states that coroners regulations may make provision:

(a) for the discharge of an investigation;
(b) for or in connection with the suspension or resumption of investigations;
(c) for the delegation by a coroner, area coroner or assistant coroner of any of his functions;
(d) allowing information to be disclosed or requiring information to be given;
(e) giving the Lord Chancellor or the Chief Coroner power to require information from coroners;
(f) requiring a summary of specified information given to the Chief Coroner by virtue of paragraph (e) to be included in reports under s.36;
(g) with respect to the prevention, retention, release or disposal of bodies;
(h) in relation to authorisations under paragraph 3 of Schedule 5 or entry and search under such authorisations, equivalent to that made by the provisions of ss.15 and 16 of the Police and Criminal Evidence Act 1984;
(i) in relation to the power of seizure conferred by paragraph 3(4)(a) of that Schedule equivalent to that made by any provision of s.21 of the Police and Criminal Evidence Act 1984;
(j) about reports under paragraph 7 of that Schedule.

Subsection (4) states that coroners regulations may apply any provisions of coroners rules.

Treasure regulations (s.44)

Under s.44(1), the Lord Chancellor may make regulations for regulating the practice and procedure at or in connection with investigations under Part 1 concerning objects that are or may be treasure or treasure trove.

Under subsection (3), triggered treasure regulations may make provision:

(a) for the discharge of an investigation;
(b) for or in connection with the suspension or resumption of investigations;
(c) for the delegation by the Coroner for Treasure of any of his or her functions;
(d) allowing information to be disclosed or requiring information to be given;
(e) giving to the Lord Chancellor or the Chief Coroner power to require information from the Coroner for Treasure;
(f) requiring a summary of specified information given to the Chief Coroner by virtue of paragraph (e) to be included in reports under s.36;
(g) of the kind mentioned in paragraph (h) or (i) of s.43(3).

Coroners rules (s.45)

Section 45(1) enables rules to be made in accordance with Part 1 of Schedule 1 to the Constitutional Reform Act 2005 for regulating the practice and procedure at or in connection with inquests, as to the way in which and the time within which appeals are to be brought and for regulating the practice and procedure at or in connection with appeals.

Subsection (2) states that coroners rules may make provision:

(a) about evidence;
(b) for the discharge of a jury;
(c) for the discharge of an inquest;
(d) for or in connection with the adjournment or resumption of inquests;
(e) for a coroner to have power to give a direction, in proceedings at an inquest, allowing or requiring a name or other matter not to be disclosed except to persons specified in that direction;
(f) for the delegation by a coroner, area coroner or assistant coroner or Coroner for Treasure of any of his functions, except for functions that involve making judicial decisions or exercising any judicial discretion;
(g) with respect to the disclosure of information;
(h) for persons to be excused from service as jurors at inquests in cases specified in the rules;
(i) as to the matters to be taken into account by the Coroner for Treasure in deciding whether to hold an inquest concerning an object that is or may be treasure or treasure trove;
(j) for requiring permission to be given in order for an appeal to be made to the Court of Appeal.

Subsection (3) has caused disquiet in that it has the effect of allowing an inquest or part thereof to be held behind closed doors. Critics are concerned that this does not permit justice to be seen to be done.

Under s.45(3), coroners rules may make provision conferring power on a coroner or Coroner for Treasure to give a direction excluding specified persons from an inquest or part of an inquest if, in the interests of national security, or to give a direction excluding specified persons from an inquest during the giving of evidence by a witness under the age of 18 if the coroner believes that will improve the quality of the witness's evidence.

2.8.2 Coroner of the Queen's household

Abolition of the office of coroner of the Queen's household (s.46)

The office of coroner of the Queen's household is abolished.

2.8.3 Interpretation

'Interested person' (s.47)

Under coronial legislation only interested persons are entitled to participate in inquests by asking questions, lodging appeals, etc. It is therefore imperative for practitioners to understand the definition of interested persons under the Act. In comparison with the old law, it will be noted that the scope of persons classed as interested persons is greatly extended.

Section 47(2) defines 'interested person' as:

(a) a spouse, civil partner, partner, parent, child, brother, sister, grandparent, grandchild, child of a brother or sister, stepfather, stepmother, half- brother or half-sister;
(b) a personal representative of the deceased;
(c) a medical examiner exercising functions in relation to the death of the deceased;
(d) a beneficiary under a life insurance policy of the deceased;
(e) the insurer who issued such a policy;
(f) a person who may 'by any act or omission have caused or contributed to the death of the deceased, or whose employee or agent may have done so';
(g) the representative of a trade union of which the deceased was a member at the time of death if the death has been caused by an injury received in the course of employment or a prescribed industrial disease;
(h) a person appointed by or representative of an enforcing authority;
(i) a Chief Constable (under s.47(3));
(j) a Provost Marshall (under s.47(4));
(k) the Independent Police Complaints Commission (under s.47(5));
(l) a person appointed by a government department to attend an inquest into the death or to assist in, or provide evidence for the purpose of, an investigation into the death under Part 1; or
(m) any other person who the coroner thinks has a sufficient interest.

An example of s.47(2)(f) could be a co-worker who started up a machine that the deceased was working upon.

Practitioners should not forget s.47(2)(m) which gives the coroner discretion to allow any person to be an interested person if he thinks they have sufficient interest. An example might be a close family friend.

Section 47(3) applies where it appears that a person has or may have committed a homicide offence involving the death of the deceased or a related offence.

Subsection (4) applies where it appears that a person has or may have committed the service equivalent of a homicide offence involving the death of the deceased or a service offence that is a related offence.

Subsection (5) applies where the death of the deceased is or has been the subject of an investigation involving the Independent Police Complaints Commission.

Subsection (6) states that an interested person in relation to an object that is or may be treasure or treasure trove, or an investigation or inquest under Chapter 4 concerning such object means:

(a) the British Museum, if the object is found (or believed to have been found) in England;
(b) the National Museum of Wales if the object is found in Wales;
(c) the finder of the object or any person otherwise involved in the find;
(d) the occupier, at the time the object was found, of the land where it was found;
(e) a person who had an interest in the land at the time or has had such an interest since;
(f) any other person who the Coroner for Treasure thinks has a sufficient interest.

Under subsection (7), for the purpose of s.47, a person is the partner of a deceased person if the two of them (whether of different sexes or the same sex) were living as partners in an enduring relationship at the time of the deceased person's death.

Interpretation: general (s.48)

Section 48(1) deals with definitions of words and phrases used within the Act. The definitions are not repeated in full here. However, some of the more common and/or important definitions are as follows:

> 'the 1953 Act' means the Births and Deaths Registration Act 1953;
>
> 'the 1988 Act' means the Coroners Act 1988;
>
> ...
>
> 'area', in relation to a senior coroner, area coroner or assistant coroner, means the coroner area for which that coroner is appointed;
>
> ...
>
> 'functions' includes powers and duties;
>
> ...

Subsection (2) states that a person is in state detention if he is 'compulsorily detained by a public authority within the meaning of section 6 of the Human Rights Act 1998'.

2.8.4 Northern Ireland and Scotland amendments

Amendments to the Coroners Act (Northern Ireland) 1959 (s.49)

Schedule 11 inserts provisions into the Coroners Act (Northern Ireland) 1959 which correspond to certain provisions in Schedules 5 and 6.

Amendments to the Fatal Accidents and Sudden Deaths Inquiry (Scotland) Act 1976 (s.50)

Under s.50(2), a new s.1A is inserted into the Fatal Accidents and Sudden Deaths Inquiry (Scotland) Act 1976 which deals with the death of service personnel abroad.

2.8.5 Amendments of Access to Justice Act 1999

Public funding for advocacy at certain inquests (s.51)

Under s.51, Schedule 2 to the Access to Justice Act 1999 is amended to provide for public funding for advocacy at inquests into the death of a person who, at the time of death:

(a) was detained at a custodial institution or in a custody area at a court or police station,

(b) was detained at a removal centre or short-term holding centre,

(c) was being transferred or held in pursuance of prison escort arrangements or immigration escort arrangements,

(d) was detained in secure accommodation,

(e) was a detained patient, or

(f) was in service custody.

2.9 PART 9: GENERAL

2.9.1 Orders, regulations and rules (s.176)

Section 176(1) states that '[o]rders or regulations made by the Secretary of State, the Lord Chancellor, the Welsh Ministers or the Chief Coroner under this Act are to be made by statutory instrument'.

2.9.2 Consequential etc. amendments and transitional and saving provisions (s.177)

Section 177(1) states that Schedule 21 contains 'minor and consequential amendments'. Subsection (2) goes on to state that Schedule 22 contains 'transitional, transitory and saving provisions'.

2.9.3 Repeals (s.178)

Section 178 states that Schedule 23 contains repeals.

2.9.4 Extent (s.181)

Subsection (1) states that subject to s.181, the Act extends to England and Wales only.

2.9.5 Commencement (s.182)

It is important to be aware that the commencement details outlined below are those that relate to the coronial aspects of the Act.

(1) The following provisions come into force on the day on which this Act is passed –

(a) sections 47 and 48;

...

(f) this section and sections 176, 177(3) to (10), 179, 181 and 183;

...

(h) paragraphs 62(3) and 94 to 98 of Schedule 21 (and section 177(1) so far as relating to those provisions);

(i) Part 1 and paragraphs 26 and 47 of Schedule 22 (and section 177(2) so far as relating to those provisions);

...

(4) The following provisions come into force on such day as the Lord Chancellor may by order appoint –

(a) Part 1 (other than sections 19, 20, 21, 47 and 48);

...

(e) Part ... 1 ... of Schedule 21 (and section 177(1) so far as relating to those provisions);

...

(g) in Schedule 23
(i) the repeals in Part 1, ...

and section 178 so far as relating to those repeals.

(5) The other provisions of this Act come into force on such day as the Secretary of State may by order appoint.

2.9.6 Short title

This section states that the Act is to be cited as the Coroners and Justice Act 2009.

2.10 SCHEDULE 1: DUTY OR POWER TO SUSPEND OR RESUME INVESTIGATIONS

2.10.1 Part 1: Suspension of investigations

Suspension where certain criminal charges may be brought

Under paragraph 1 a coroner must suspend an investigation under the Act where:

- a prosecuting authority requests the coroner to suspend the investigation on the grounds that a person may be charged with a homicide offence involving the death of the deceased or an offence, other than a service offence, that is alleged to be a related offence; or where
- a Provost Marshall or the Director of Service Prosecutions requests the coroner to suspend investigations on the ground that a person may be charged with the service equivalent of a homicide offence involving the deceased or a service offence that is alleged to be a related offence.

Paragraph 1(6) defines the meaning of 'homicide offence'. Practitioners should be familiar with this part of the Schedule as it includes not only the anticipated offences of murder, manslaughter, etc. but also other offences including encouraging or assisting suicide, and causing death by dangerous driving.

Suspension where certain criminal proceedings are brought

Under paragraph 2 a coroner must suspend an investigation under the Act where:

- he becomes aware that a person has appeared or been brought before a magistrates' court charged with a homicide offence involving the deceased or that a person has been charged on an indictment with such an offence;
- he becomes aware that a person has been charged with the service equivalent of a homicide offence involving the deceased;
- a prosecuting authority informs the coroner that a person has appeared or been brought before a magistrates' court charged with an offence (other than a service offence) that is alleged to be a related offence or has been charged on an indictment with such an offence and a prosecuting authority requests the coroner to suspend the investigation; or
- the Director of Service Prosecutions informs the coroner that a person has been charged with a service offence that is alleged to be a related offence and requests that the investigation is suspended.

Suspension pending inquiry under Inquiries Act 2005

Under paragraph 3(1) a coroner must suspend an investigation into a person's death under the Act if the Lord Chancellor so requests on the grounds that the cause of death is likely to be adequately investigated by an inquiry that is being, or is to be, held under Inquiries Act 2005 and that a senior judge has been appointed under that Act as chairman of the inquiry.

It is clarified at paragraph 4(2) that the 'terms of reference of the inquiry must be such that it has as its purpose, or among its purposes, the purpose set out in section 5(1) above … ; and section 5 of the Inquiries Act 2005 has effect accordingly'.

General power to suspend

Under paragraph 5, a coroner may suspend an investigation under the Act if it appears to the coroner 'that it would be appropriate to do so'.

Effect of suspension

Paragraph 6 states that where an investigation is suspended under Schedule 1, the coroner must adjourn any inquest that is being held as part of the investigation and that the coroner may also discharge the jury.

2.10.2 Part 2: Resumption of investigations

Resumption of investigations suspended under paragraph 1

Paragraph 7 states that an investigation that is suspended under paragraph 1 must be resumed once a prescribed period under that paragraph has elapsed.

Resumption of investigations suspended under paragraph 2

Under paragraph 8, an investigation that is suspended under paragraph 2 may not be resumed unless the coroner 'thinks that there is sufficient reason for resuming it'.

Any investigation that is suspended under paragraph 2 may not be resumed whilst proceedings are continuing unless the relevant prosecuting authority confirms that it has no objection.

In the case of an investigation resumed under this paragraph, a determination may not be inconsistent with the outcome of the criminal proceedings.

Resumption of investigations suspended under paragraph 3

Under paragraph 9(1) where an investigation is suspended under paragraph 3, it may not be resumed unless the coroner 'thinks that there is sufficient reason for resuming it'. It must not be resumed before the end of the period of 28 days beginning with the relevant day. Further, it may not be resumed in certain circumstances where subparagraphs (4), (6), (8) or (10) apply.

The 'relevant day' means the day on which the inquiry concerned is concluded, if the Lord Chancellor gives notification to that effect, or the day on which the findings of the inquiry are published.

Subparagraph (4) applies where, during the suspension of the investigation, the coroner becomes aware that a person has appeared or been brought before a magistrates' court charged with a homicide offence regarding the deceased or becomes aware that a person has been charged on an indictment with such an offence.

Subparagraph (6) applies where, during the suspension of the investigation, the coroner becomes aware that a person has been charged with the service equivalent of a homicide offence involving the death of the deceased. This subparagraph also states that the coroner must not resume the investigation until after the conclusion of proceedings before the court of trial in respect of the offence in question.

Subparagraph (8) applies where, during the suspension of the investigation, a prosecuting authority informs the coroner that a person has appeared or been brought before a magistrates' court charged with an offence (other than a service offence) that is alleged to be a related offence or has been charged on an indictment with such an offence.

Subparagraph (10) applies where the Director of Service Prosecutions informs the coroner that a person has been charged with a service offence that is alleged to be a related offence.

Where subparagraphs (4), (6), (8) or (10) apply, the coroner will not resume the investigation until after the conclusion of the criminal proceedings unless the prosecuting authority confirms that it has no objection.

Resumption of investigation suspended under paragraph 5

Paragraph 10 states that 'An investigation that is suspended under paragraph 5 may be resumed at any time if the senior coroner thinks that there is sufficient reason for resuming it'.

Supplemental

Where an investigation is resumed under Schedule 1 then the coroner is required to resume any inquest adjourned under paragraph 6.

Under paragraph 11(4), it is outlined that where the original inquest was held with a jury and the coroner decides to resume with a jury then if at least seven persons who were members of the original jury are available, the resumed inquest must be held with a jury consisting of those persons. If not, or if the original jury was discharged, a new jury should be summoned.

2.11 SCHEDULE 2: CORONER AREAS

This is an important Schedule as it is likely that there will be some rationalisation of the existing coronial areas. However, the extent and effectiveness of the rationalisation will depend on the rules and regulations brought in to supplement the Act.

2.11.1 Coroner areas

Paragraph 1 confirms that England and Wales is to be divided into areas known as coroner areas. Each of those areas is to 'consist of the area of a local authority or the combined areas of two or more local authorities'.

Before making an order in relation to coroner areas, the Lord Chancellor is required to consult with every local authority, the Welsh Ministers and any other persons the Lord Chancellor thinks appropriate.

2.11.2 Alteration of coroner areas

Under paragraph 2, the Lord Chancellor may make orders altering coroner areas, consulting as per paragraph 1 of Schedule 2.

2.11.3 Relevant authorities

In the case of a coroner area consisting of an area of a single local authority, that authority is the relevant authority for the coroner area.

In the case of a coroner area which consists of the areas of two or more local authorities, the relevant authority is whichever one of those authorities they jointly nominate or, if they cannot agree, whichever one the Lord Chancellor determines.

2.11.4 Effect of body being outside coroner area etc.

Paragraph 4 applies where a coroner is responsible for conducting an investigation into a death and the body is outside the coroner's area.

In such circumstances, the coroner 'has the same functions in relation to the body and the investigation as would be the case if the body were within the coroner's area' ... 'The presence of the body at a place outside the coroner's area does not confer any functions on any other coroner.'

2.12 SCHEDULE 3: APPOINTMENT ETC. OF SENIOR CORONERS, AREA CORONERS AND ASSISTANT CORONERS

2.12.1 Part 1: Appointment of senior, area and assistant coroners

Appointment of senior coroners

Paragraph 1 states that the relevant authority for each coroner area must appoint a coroner referred to as the 'senior coroner' for that area. A person cannot be appointed unless the Lord Chancellor and the Chief Coroner both consent to the appointment.

Appointment of area and assistant coroners

The Lord Chancellor may by order require the appointment, for any coroner area, of an area coroner, or a specified number of area coroners, or a minimum number of assistant coroners. A person may not be appointed as an area coroner or assistant coroner unless the Lord Chancellor and the Chief Coroner both consent to the appointment.

2.12.2 Part 2: Qualifications of senior, area and assistant coroners

Paragraph 3 states that to be eligible for appointment as a senior coroner, area coroner or assistant coroner, a person must be under the age of 70 and satisfy the judicial appointment eligibility condition on a five-year basis.

Paragraph 4 precludes any person from such an appointment who is a councillor for a local authority, or has been during the previous six months, for a coroner area that is the same as or includes the area of that local authority.

2.12.3 Part 3: Vacancies; functions of area and assistant coroners

Filling of vacancies

Subsection (1) of paragraph 5 states that the paragraph applies where a vacancy occurs in the office of coroner or in the office of area coroner for an area. In such circumstances, the relevant authority for the area must:

(a) give notice in writing of the vacancy to the Lord Chancellor and the Chief Coroner as soon as possible after the vacancy occurs;
(b) appoint a person to fill the vacancy within three months of the vacancy occurring or within whatever further period the Lord Chancellor allows;
(c) give notice in writing of the appointment of a person to fill the vacancy to the Lord Chancellor and the Chief Coroner as soon as possible after it is filled.

Paragraph 6 applies where a vacancy occurs in an office of assistant coroner for an area and the vacancy causes the number of assistant coroners for the area to fall below the minimum number specified.

Within three months of such a vacancy occurring, or within whatever further period allowed by the Lord Chancellor, the relevant authority for the coronial area must appoint a person to fill the vacancy.

Person to act as senior coroner in case of vacancy

Paragraph 7 applies where a vacancy occurs in the office of senior coroner for an area. In such circumstances, the area coroner for the area, or if there is more than one such area coroner, whichever of them is nominated by the relevant authority, is to act as coroner for the area whilst the vacancy remain.

Where there is no area coroner for the area, an assistant coroner for the area who is nominated by the relevant authority for the area, is to act as senior coroner for the area whilst the vacancy remains.

For the sake of clarity, paragraph 7(5) states that a person who acts as senior coroner under these circumstances is to be treated for all purposes of the Act as being senior coroner for the area.

Functions of area and assistant coroners

Paragraph 8 states that an area coroner or assistant coroner for an area may perform any functions of the senior coroner for that area during any period when that senior coroner is absent or unavailable, or at any other time, with the consent of that senior coroner.

Accordingly, a reference to a senior coroner in any statutory provision is 'to be read, where appropriate, as including an area coroner or assistant coroner'.

2.12.4 Part 4: Terms of office of senior, area and assistant coroners

Status of office

Paragraph 9 states that the 'offices of senior coroner, area coroner and assistant coroner are not to be regarded as freehold offices'.

Vacation or termination of office

Paragraph 10 states that a senior coroner, area coroner or assistant coroner 'must vacate office on reaching the age of 70'.

Paragraph 11 makes it clear that a senior coroner, area coroner or assistant coroner must vacate office immediately if he or she becomes a councillor for a local authority and the area of that local authority is the same as, or falls within, the relevant coroner area.

Paragraph 12 states that the senior coroner, area coroner or assistant coroner for an area may resign from office by giving notice in writing to the relevant authority for the area. The resignation however, does not take effect unless and until it is accepted by the authority.

Paragraph 13 enables the Lord Chancellor, with the agreement of the Lord Chief Justice, to remove a senior coroner, area coroner or assistant coroner from that office for incapacity or misbehaviour.

Discipline

Paragraph 14 ensures that Chapter 3 of Part 4 of the Constitutional Reform Act 2005 applies in relation to the offices of senior coroner, area coroner and assistant coroner.

Salary of senior and area coroners

Paragraph 15 states that the senior coroner for an area is entitled to a salary and that '[t]he amount of the salary is to be whatever is from time to time agreed by the senior coroner and the relevant authority for the area'.

If the senior coroner and the relevant authority are unable to agree about an alteration in the level of salary then either may refer the matter to the Lord Chancellor who may determine the amount and the date on which it is to become payable.

The same provisions apply in relation to an area coroner.

Many critics argue that the Act has missed a chance to ensure central funding for the coronial system. It is argued that whilst funding is provided by local authorities on a regional basis, this inevitably leads to disparity and criticisms of a postcode lottery.

There is a danger of this concern becoming self-fulfilling with the most able coroners being attracted to the best paying coroner areas. It could be argued that a standardised national coronial service would have removed this risk.

Fees payable to assistants

Paragraph 16 states that an assistant coroner for an area is entitled to fees. The level of fees is to be 'whatever is agreed from time to time by the assistant coroner and the relevant authority for the area'.

Again, as funding has not been centralised, the same criticisms apply as mentioned in relation to paragraph 15.

Pensions for senior and area coroners

Paragraph 17 states that a 'relevant authority for a coroner area must make provision for the payment of pensions, allowances or gratuities to or in respect of persons who are or have been senior coroners or area coroners for the area'.

It should be noted that no such requirement is in place in relation to assistant coroners.

Prohibition on receipt of fees etc.

Under paragraph 18, '[e]xcept as permitted under this or any other Act, a senior coroner, area coroner or assistant coroner may not accept any remuneration or fee in respect of anything done by that coroner in the performance of his or her functions'.

This section is clearly aimed at ensuring the independence of the office of coroner and ensuring that the office is not tainted by any outside remuneration of any sort.

Other terms of office

Paragraph 19 confirms that the senior coroner, area coroner or assistant coroner 'for an area holds office on whatever terms are from time to time agreed by that coroner and the relevant authority for the area'.

2.13 SCHEDULE 4: CORONER FOR TREASURE AND ASSISTANT CORONERS FOR TREASURE

2.13.1 Part 1: Appointment, qualifications and terms of office of Coroner for Treasure

Appointment

Under paragraph 1, the Lord Chancellor is empowered to appoint a person as the Coroner for Treasure.

Qualifications

To be eligible, a person must be under the age of 70 and satisfy the judicial-appointment eligibility condition on a five-year basis.

Vacation or termination of office

Under paragraph 3, it is made clear that the Coroner for Treasure must vacate office on reaching the age of 70.

Under paragraph 4 the Coroner for Treasure may resign by giving notice to the Lord Chancellor but this does not take effect until accepted by the Lord Chancellor.

Under paragraph 5, the Lord Chancellor, with agreement of the Lord Chief Justice, may remove the Coroner for Treasure from office for incapacity or misbehaviour.

Remuneration, allowances and expenses

Under paragraph 6, the Lord Chancellor may pay to the Coroner for Treasure amounts determined by the Lord Chancellor by way of remuneration or allowances.

2.13.2 Part 2: Designation and remuneration of Assistant Coroners for Treasure

Designation

Under paragraph 7, the Chief Coroner may designate one or more assistant coroners to act as Assistant Coroners for Treasure.

Remuneration, allowances and expenses

Under paragraph 10, it is stated that '[t]he Lord Chancellor may pay to an Assistant Coroner for Treasure amounts determined by the Lord Chancellor by way of remuneration or allowances'.

2.13.3 Part 3: Miscellaneous

Functions of Assistant Coroners for Treasure

Under paragraph 11, an Assistant Coroner for Treasure may perform any functions of the Coroner for Treasure:

(a) during a period when the Coroner for Treasure is absent;
(b) during any vacancy in the office of Coroner for Treasure;
(c) at any other time, with the consent of the Coroner for Treasure.

Staff

Under paragraph 12, the 'Lord Chancellor may appoint staff to assist the Coroner for Treasure and any Assistant Coroners for Treasure in the performance of their functions'.

2.14 SCHEDULE 5: POWERS OF CORONERS

2.14.1 Power to require evidence to be given or produced

Paragraph 1(1) enables the coroner to require a person to attend and give evidence at an inquest, produce documents or produce any other thing relevant to an inquest. Paragraph 1(2) goes on to enable the coroner to issue a notice requiring a person to provide evidence in the form of a written statement, produce documents or produce any other thing to assist in conduct an investigation. In either case the notice must explain the possible consequences of not complying with the request.

Under paragraph 2, a person may not be required to give, produce or provide any evidence or document if he could not be required to do so in civil proceedings or the requirement 'would be incompatible with a Community obligation'.

2.14.2 Power of entry, search and seizure

Paragraph 3(1) enables a coroner to enter and search any land specified in an authorisation, if authorised in writing by the Chief Coroner or another coroner nominated by the Chief Coroner.

Paragraph 3(2) states that such an authorisation will only be given if the coroner conducting the investigation has reason to suspect that there may be anything on the land which relates to a matter relevant to the investigation and any of the conditions in subparagraph (3) are met.

The conditions in subparagraph (3) are:

(a) that it is not practicable to communicate with a person entitled to grant permission to enter and search the land;

(b) that permission to enter and search the land has been refused;

(c) that the senior coroner has reason to believe that such permission would be refused if requested;

(d) that the purpose of a search may be frustrated or seriously prejudiced unless the senior coroner can secure immediate entry to the land on arrival.

The power of seizure does not apply to any item that the person searching believes is subject to legal privilege.

2.14.3 Exhumation of body for examination

Under paragraph 6 a coroner may order the exhumation of a body if either:

- the body is buried in England and Wales and the coroner thinks it necessary for the body to be examined under s.14; or
- the body is buried within the coroner area for which the coroner is appointed and he believes it necessary for the body to be examined for the purpose of any criminal proceedings that have been instituted or contemplated.

2.14.4 Action to prevent other deaths

Under paragraph 7, where a coroner has been conducting an investigation into a person's death and this give rise to a concern that other deaths may occur, the coroner may report the matter to a person who the coroner believes may have power to take action to eliminate or reduce such a risk.

A person to whom the coroner makes a report under this paragraph must give the coroner a written response to it.

2.15 SCHEDULE 6: OFFENCES

2.15.1 Part 1: Offences relating to jurors

Paragraph 1 makes it an offence for a person to serve on a jury at an inquest if they are disqualified from jury service and know that they are disqualified. Such a person is liable on summary conviction to a fine not exceeding level 5 on the standard scale.

Paragraph 2 makes it an offence for a person to refuse without reasonable excuse to answer any question put, to give an answer knowing it to be false or to recklessly give an answer that is false in a material particular. Such a person is liable on summary conviction to a fine not exceeding level 3 on the standard scale.

Paragraph 3 makes it an offence for a person summoned as a juror at an inquest to make any false representation or cause or permit any false representation to be made with the intention of evading service as a juror. Such a person is liable on summary conviction to a fine not exceeding level 3 on the standard scale.

Paragraph 4 makes it an offence for a person to make or cause to be made on behalf of a person summoned as a juror at an inquest, any false representation with the intention of enabling the other person to evade service. Such a person is liable on summary conviction to a fine not exceeding level 3 on the standard scale.

Paragraph 5 enables a coroner to impose a fine not exceeding £1,000 on a person duly summoned as a juror at an inquest who fails without reasonable excuse to attend, or attends but refuses without reasonable excuse to serve as a juror. A fine may not be imposed unless a summons was duly served not later than 14 days before the day on which the person was required to attend.

2.15.2 Part 2: Offences relating to witnesses and evidence

Paragraph 6 enables a coroner to impose a fine not exceeding £1,000 on any person 'who fails without reasonable excuse to do anything required by a notice under paragraph 1 of Schedule 5'.

Paragraph 7(1) makes it an offence for a person to do anything that is intended to have the effect of distorting or otherwise altering any evidence, or preventing any evidence being given, produced or provided, or do anything likely to have that effect.

Paragraph 7(2) makes it an offence for a person to intentionally suppress or conceal a document known to be relevant, or intentionally alter or destroy such a document.

A person guilty of an offence under paragraph 7(1) or (2) is liable on summary conviction to a fine not exceeding level 3 on the standard scale or imprisonment for a term not exceeding 51 weeks or to both.

Paragraph 8(1) makes it an offence for a person giving unsworn evidence at an inquest 'to give false evidence in such circumstances that, had the evidence been given on oath, he or she would have been guilty of perjury'. A person guilty of such an offence is liable on summary conviction to a fine not exceeding £1,000 or to imprisonment for a term not exceeding 51 weeks or to both. If the person is under the age of 14, the fine must not exceed £250.

2.15.3 Part 3: Miscellaneous

Paragraph 9 states that the powers of a coroner under paragraph 5 or 6 are additional to any other power the coroner may have to:

- compel a person to appear before him;
- compel a person to give evidence or produce a document or thing; or
- punish a person for contempt of court for failure to appear or give evidence or to produce any document or thing.

However, a person may not be fined under paragraph 5 or 6 and also be punished under any such other power.

2.16 SCHEDULE 7: ALLOWANCES, FEES AND EXPENSES

2.16.1 Part 1: Allowances payable to jurors

Paragraph 1 states the person who serves as a juror at an inquest is entitled to receive payments by way of allowance for travelling and subsistence and for financial loss.

Paragraph 2 states that payment for financial loss will only be made if the person has incurred expenses, suffered a loss of earnings or suffered a loss of benefit that he would not have incurred otherwise.

2.16.2 Part 2: Allowances payable to witnesses

Paragraph 5(1) states that regulations may prescribe the allowances that may be paid to witnesses, persons who produce documents or things, or persons who provide evidence in the form of a written statement. Subparagraph (2) clarifies that 'witness' does not include a police officer, a prison officer or a prisoner.

2.16.3 Part 3: Miscellaneous fees, allowances and expenses

Paragraph 6 states that the regulations may prescribe fees and allowances that may be paid by a coroner to persons who make examinations under s.14.

Paragraph 7(1) permits a relevant authority to issue a schedule of the fees, allowances and expenses that may be paid.

2.16.4 Part 4: Meeting or reimbursing expenses

Paragraph 9 permits regulations to make provision for meeting or reimbursing expenses incurred by coroners, area coroners and assistant coroners and expenses incurred by virtue of Schedule 10 in the conduct of an investigation by the Chief Coroner, Coroner for Treasure or by a judge or former coroner.

2.16.5 Part 5: Supplemental

Paragraph 10 states that for the purposes of paragraph 1 of this Schedule, 'a person who attends for service as a juror in accordance with a summons is to be treated as serving as a juror even if he or she is not sworn'.

2.17 SCHEDULE 8: CHIEF CORONER AND DEPUTY CHIEF CORONERS

2.17.1 Appointment of Chief Coroner

Paragraph 1(1) states that the Lord Chief Justice may appoint a person to the office of Chief Coroner. To be eligible for appointment as the Chief Coroner, a person must be a judge of the High Court or a circuit judge and under the age of 70.

Paragraph 1(4) states the appointment is to be for a term decided by the Lord Chief Justice after consulting with the Lord Chancellor.

2.17.2 Appointment of Deputy Chief Coroners

Under paragraph 2, the 'Lord Chief Justice may secure the appointment as Deputy Chief Coroners of however many persons the Lord Chief Justice thinks appropriate'. Paragraph 2(2) goes on to specify that to be eligible for appointment as a Deputy Chief Coroner, a person must be a judge of the High Court or a circuit judge, the Coroner for Treasure or a coroner and under the age of 70.

2.17.3 Resignation or removal

Paragraph 3 states that the Chief Coroner or a Deputy Chief Coroner may resign from office by giving notice in writing to the Lord Chief Justice. However, the resignation does not take effect 'unless and until is accepted by the Lord Chief Justice' who must consult the Lord Chancellor before accepting it.

Paragraph 4 permits the Lord Chief Justice, after consultation with the Lord Chancellor, to remove the Chief Coroner or a Deputy Chief Coroner from office for incapacity or misbehaviour.

2.17.4 Remuneration, allowances and expenses

Paragraph 5 permits the Lord Chancellor to pay the Chief Coroner amounts by way of remuneration or allowances, and amounts towards expenses incurred by the Chief Coroner in performing his functions.

Paragraph 6 permits the Lord Chancellor to pay a Deputy Chief Coroner amounts by way of remuneration or allowances, and amounts towards expenses incurred by that Deputy Chief Coroner in performing his functions.

2.17.5 Exercise of Chief Coroner's functions by Deputy Chief Coroner

A Deputy Chief Coroner may perform any functions of the Chief Coroner during a period when the Chief Coroner is absent or unavailable, during a vacancy in the office of Chief Coroner or at any other time with the consent of the Chief Coroner.

2.17.6 Staff

Paragraph 9 requires the Lord Chancellor to 'appoint staff to assist the Chief Coroner and any Deputy Chief Coroners in the performance of their functions'.

2.18 SCHEDULE 9: MEDICAL ADVISER AND DEPUTY MEDICAL ADVISERS TO THE CHIEF CORONER

2.18.1 Appointment and functions of the Medical Adviser to the Chief Coroner

Under paragraph 1, the Lord Chancellor may appoint a person as Medical Adviser to the Chief Coroner to provide advice and assistance to the Chief Coroner on medical matters in relation to the coroner system.

2.18.2 Appointment and functions of Deputy Medical Advisers to the Chief Coroner

Under paragraph 2, the Lord Chancellor may appoint however many Deputy Medical Advisers to the Chief Coroner as he thinks appropriate. Under paragraph 2(2), a Deputy Medical Adviser may perform the functions of the Medical Adviser:

(a) during a period when the Medical Adviser is absent or unavailable;

(b) during a vacancy in the office of Medical Adviser;

(c) at any other time, with the consent of the Medical Adviser.

2.18.3 Qualifications for appointment

Under paragraph 3, a person is qualified to be appointed as the Medical Adviser or as a Deputy Medical Adviser if he or she is a registered medical practitioner and has been such for five years, and practises as such or has done within the previous five years.

2.18.4 Consultation before making appointment

Before appointing a Medical Adviser or a Deputy Medical Adviser, the Lord Chancellor must consult the Chief Coroner and the Welsh Ministers.

2.18.5 Terms and conditions of appointment

The appointment of Medical Adviser or Deputy Medical Adviser 'is to be on whatever terms and conditions the Lord Chancellor thinks appropriate'.

2.18.6 Remuneration, allowances and expenses

Under paragraph 6, the Lord Chancellor may pay the Medical Adviser and Deputy Medical Advisers amounts for remuneration, allowances and expenses.

2.19 SCHEDULE 10: INVESTIGATION BY CHIEF CORONER OR CORONER FOR TREASURE OR BY JUDGE, FORMER JUDGE OR FORMER CORONER

2.19.1 Investigation by Chief Coroner

Paragraph 1(1) enables the Chief Coroner to conduct an investigation into a person's death. Where this occurs, the Chief Coroner has the same functions as if he were the coroner for the area in which the body was situated. In these circumstances, no coroner, area coroner or assistant coroner has any functions in relation to the body or the investigation.

2.19.2 Investigation by Coroner for Treasure

Paragraph 2(1) enables the Chief Coroner to direct the Coroner for Treasure to conduct an investigation into a person's death. Where this occurs, the Coroner for Treasure has the same functions as if he were the coroner for the area in which the body was situated. In these circumstances, no coroner, area coroner or assistant coroner has any functions in relation to the body or the investigation.

2.19.3 Investigation by judge, former judge or former coroner

Under paragraph 3 the Chief Coroner may request the Lord Chief Justice to nominate a judge of the High Court or a circuit judge or a person who has held the office of judge or a former coroner to conduct an investigation into a person's death. Where this paragraph applies, the judge has the same functions in relation to the body and the investigation as would be the case if he or she were a coroner in whose area the body was situated. In these circumstances, no coroner, area coroner or assistant coroner has any functions in relation to the body or the investigation.

2.19.4 Appeals

Under paragraph 4(1) where an investigation is conducted by a judge of the High Court or by a person who has held office as judge of the Court of Appeal and the investigation gives rise to an appeal under s.40, that section has effect as if references to the Chief Coroner were references to the Court of Appeal.

Under paragraph 4(2) where an investigation is conducted by a circuit judge and the investigation gives rise to an appeal under s.40, that section has effect as if references to the Chief Coroner were references to a judge of the High Court.

2.19.5 Investigations already begun

Paragraph 5 makes it clear that a 'reference in this Schedule to conducting an investigation, in the case of an investigation that has already begun, is to be read as a reference to continuing to conduct the investigation'.

2.20 SCHEDULE 11: AMENDMENTS TO THE CORONERS ACT (NORTHERN IRELAND) 1959

2.20.1 Witnesses and evidence

Paragraph 1 provides some substitutions to s.17 (Witnesses to be summoned) of the Coroners Act (Northern Ireland) 1959.

These are:

- 17A Power to require evidence to be given or produced;
- 17B Giving or producing evidence: further provision;
- 17C Offences relating to evidence.

2.21 SCHEDULE 21: MINOR AND CONSEQUENTIAL AMENDMENTS

2.21.1 Part 1: Coroners etc.

Part 1 provides amendments to the following:

- Cremation Act 1902 – dealt with by paragraph 1;
- Births and Deaths Registration Act 1926 – dealt with by paragraphs 2 to 4 inclusive;
- Visiting Forces Act 1952 – dealt with by paragraph 5;
- Births and Deaths Registration Act 1953 – dealt with by paragraphs 6 to 21 inclusive;
- Courts Act 1971 – dealt with by paragraph 22;
- Pensions (Increase) Act 1971 – dealt with by paragraph 23;
- Juries Act 1974 – dealt with by paragraph 24;
- Health and Safety at Work etc. Act 1974 – dealt with by paragraph 25;
- House of Commons Disqualification Act 1975 – dealt with by paragraph 26;
- Northern Ireland Assembly Disqualification Act 1975 – dealt with by paragraph 27;
- Magistrates' Courts Act 1980 – dealt with by paragraph 28;
- Access to Health Records Act 1990 – dealt with by paragraph 29;
- Courts and Legal Services Act 1990 – dealt with by paragraph 30;
- Judicial Pensions and Retirement Act 1993 – dealt with by paragraph 31;
- Merchant Shipping Act 1995 – dealt with by paragraphs 32 to 35 inclusive;
- Employment Rights Act 1996 – dealt with by paragraph 36;
- Treasure Act 1996 – dealt with by paragraphs 37 to 42 inclusive;
- Northern Ireland (Location of Victims' Remains) Act 1999 – dealt with by paragraph 43;
- Freedom of Information Act 2000 – dealt with by paragraph 44;
- International Criminal Court Act 2001 – dealt with by paragraph 45;
- Courts Act 2003 – dealt with by paragraph 46;

- Human Tissue Act 2004 – dealt with by paragraphs 47 to 50 inclusive;
- Constitutional Reform Act 2005 – dealt with by paragraph 51.

2.22 SCHEDULE 22: TRANSITIONAL, TRANSITORY AND SAVING PROVISIONS

2.22.1 Part 1: Coroners etc.

Coroner areas

Paragraph 1 requires the Lord Chancellor to make an order specifying as a coroner area the area of each coroner's district immediately before the repeal and the area coming into force at the same time as the repeal. This is to be known as the 'transitional order'.

Relevant authorities

For the purpose of Part 1 of Schedule 22, the 'relevant authority' for each coroner area specified in the transitional order is the authority that was the relevant council under the Coroners Act 1988 for the corresponding coroner's district.

Senior and assistant coroners

Paragraph 3(2) confirms that a person who immediately before the repeal was the coroner for a district and, but for the repeal, would have continued in that office, is to be treated as having been appointed as the senior coroner for the corresponding coroner area.

Paragraph 3(3) provides the same 'grandfather rights' for deputy and assistant deputy coroners.

Coroner for Treasure

Paragraph 4 confirms that in 'the case of the first appointment to the office of Coroner for Treasure, paragraph 2(b) of Schedule 4 does not apply to a person holding office as a coroner, deputy coroner, or assistant deputy coroner' under the Coroners Act 1988.

Investigation by former coroner

A person who was appointed a coroner under s.1 of the Coroners Act 1988 and ceased to hold office as such before the coming into force of the repeal by this Act is to be treated for the purposes of paragraph 3(3) of Schedule 10 as having held office as senior coroner.

Interpretation

Paragraph 6 states that in this Part:

> 'the 1988 Act' means the Coroners Act 1988;
>
> 'coroner's district' or 'district' means a coroner's district for the purposes of the 1988 Act;
>
> 'corresponding coroner area' (in relation to a district, means the coroner area that by virtue of the transitional order) has the same area as that district;
>
> 'corresponding coroner's district' (in relation to a coroner area, means the coroner's district whose area becomes by virtue of the transitional order) the area of that coroner area;
>
> 'transitional order' means the order made by virtue of paragraph 1(1).

2.23 SCHEDULE 23: REPEALS

2.23.1 Part 1: Coroners etc.

This Part deals with which Acts or parts of Acts have been repealed by the Coroners and Justice Act 2009. The repeals are as follows:

- Births and Deaths Registration Act 1953 – in s.20, from 'at any time' to 'of any person', s.21, s.23A(6), in s.29 (4)(b) and the 'or' preceding it, and s.34(4);
- Coroners Act (Northern Ireland) 1959 – ss.19 and 20.
- Juries Act 1974 – s.22(1);
- Magistrates' Courts Act 1980 – in Sched. 6A, the entry relating to the Coroners Act 1988;
- Coroners Act 1988 – the whole Act;.
- Caldey Island Act 1990 – s.3 and s.4(1)(c);
- Local Government (Wales) Act 1994 – in Sched.17, para.23;
- Treasure Act 1996 – s.13.
- Access to Justice Act 1999 – ss.71 and 104(1). In Sched.2, in para.2, the 'and' following para.3;
- Regional Assemblies (Preparations) Act 2003 – in the Sched, para.2.
- Courts Act 2003 – in Sched.8, para.302;
- Criminal Justice Act 2003 – in Sched.3, para.59;
- Domestic Violence, Crime and Victims Act 2004 – in Sched.10, paras.26 and 27.
- Human Tissue Act 2004 – in Sched.6, para.3.
- Constitutional Reform Act 2005 – in Sched.1, paras.19 to 21, in Sched.4, paras.193 to 195 and in Sched.7, in para.4, the entry in Part A relating to the Coroners Act 1988;
- Road Safety Act 2006 – ss.20(5) and 21(4);
- Armed Forces Act 2006 – in Sched.16, paras.110 and 111;
- Corporate Manslaughter and Corporate Homicide Act 2007 – in Sched.2, para.1;

- Local Government and Public Involvement in Health Act 2007 – in Sched.1, para.15.

3 COMMENTARY ON THE DRAFT CHARTER FOR BEREAVED PEOPLE

3.1 INTRODUCTION

At the stage of this book going to print, the Charter for Bereaved People (full title 'Charter for bereaved people who come into contact with a reformed coroner system') had not been finalised. However, while the charter is not part of the Act, it is so entwined with it that commentary is provided on it here for the sake of completeness. A full copy of the draft charter is set out at **Appendix 2**.

The Government's plans to reform the coroner system were first set out in detail in the draft Coroners Bill which was published in June 2006. Alongside the Bill, the Government published the first draft of the Charter for Bereaved People.

Initial consultation on the draft charter took place in 2006. The charter was generally welcomed as a step forward in the service bereaved people could expect. A further discussion paper on the charter was issued in 2008 and the final revised draft prepared in January 2009 for placing before Parliament.

A total of 84 responses were received to the consultation. Responses came from a wide variety of organisations and individuals, including coroners themselves, medical professionals, local authorities, voluntary organisations and bereaved family members. During the consultation period, the Ministry of Justice also had a number of meetings with coroners and interested voluntary groups about the charter.

Some respondents felt the draft charter focused on bereaved family members to the detriment of other interested parties such as paramedics, insurance companies and NHS Trusts. As a result, some respondents felt that the charter risked being unfair and unbalanced. Indeed, the Coroners' Society argued that it was potentially wrong to favour one set of people and that a charter should cover all interested persons.

To mitigate these concerns, the Ministry of Justice clarified that this charter is for the bereaved and they confirmed that it is their intention that guidance will be produced for other interested persons at inquests at a later stage. They have confirmed that it is not their intention that bereaved families receive preferential service, but having their own charter recognises the different and specific needs they have in comparison with other users of the coronial service.

As with the Act, the charter was largely welcomed as it clearly set out what can and should be expected by those coming into contact with, as well as working within, the coronial system.

The British Lung Foundation (BLF) issued a three-page document entitled 'The Coroners and Justice Bill: improving coroners enquiries that follow a death from mesothelioma'. They stated:

> The BLF strongly welcomes the ... Charter for the Bereaved. We believe that this represents an important step forward in addressing the multiple problems in mesothelioma investigations.

However the BLF raised the question of whether the Bill contains the necessary legislation to enforce the Charter for Bereaved People and subsequent guidance.

Whilst the charter has been largely welcomed, its success or otherwise will largely be dependent upon whether sufficient funding is made available to enable its objectives to be achieved.

Many people raised concerns about resourcing during the consultation period. Whilst the Ministry of Justice stated that they understood the concerns, they confirmed that they had no plans to alter current local authority funding arrangements for individual coroners. Therefore, some doubts must remain as to how the laudable aims of the charter will be met in practice.

The charter sets out 'best practice' for the coronial service. It is accepted that many coronial jurisdictions already operate to very high standards of service, but the charter aims to ensure a more consistent level of service irrespective of where the bereaved come into contact with the coronial service.

The charter will be enabled by legislation and will have the status of statutory guidance. It details the services that bereaved people who come into contact with a reformed coroner service can expect to receive, and sets out their rights of redress if these services are not delivered. Additionally, the charter sets out appeal rights against particular decisions taken by coroners in individual cases.

3.2 COMMENTARY ON THE CHARTER

For ease of reference, the commentary below utilises the same numbered paragraphs as are contained in the charter itself.

3.2.1 Overview

Paragraph 1 states that it is a charter for a reformed service and not for the service as it was currently structured and operated. It makes it clear that it is a charter for any family member of the person who has died and who the coroner has decided is a 'properly interested person'.

3.2.2 General

Paragraph 2 explains the circumstances in which a coroner's investigation is required, namely where the death is violent, unnatural, of unknown cause or incurred while the person is detained by the state.

Paragraph 3 sets out that the purposes of the coroner service are:

- to establish whether a coroner's investigation is required
- if so, to establish the identity of someone who has died, and how, when and where the person died
- to assist in the prevention of future deaths
- to provide public reassurance.

Some people have been concerned that this paragraph fails to set out what the service is *not* intended to do. In particular, many people coming into contact with the coroner system expect that it will deal with issues of blame when clearly that is not within its remit. An explanation of the limitations of the coroner system would have helped to manage expectations.

Paragraph 4 helpfully explains that the coroner service comprises not only HM Coroners but that the coroners are supported by coroner's officers and administrative staff.

It also states that the charter sets out the objectives of the service following reform and the rights and responsibilities of bereaved people during coronial investigations including inquests.

Paragraph 5 states that most full investigations will take between 6 and 12 months to complete but that a small number will take less time and an even smaller number will take longer. This whole paragraph was inserted in the last period of discussion. Its intention is clearly to manage expectations as to duration of investigations. Local authorities will need to ensure that there is sufficient funding in place to ensure that these expectations are met.

3.2.3 Definitions

Paragraphs 6 to 9 deal with definitions and are therefore not expanded here.

3.2.4 Objectives

Paragraph 10 sets out the objectives for the coroner's office in the reformed coroner service. Eight objectives are set out as being to:

- help bereaved people understand the cause of the death of the person who has died
- inform bereaved people about the role and powers of the coroner
- inform bereaved people of their rights and responsibilities if a coroner's investigation is conducted in relation to the death
- take account, where possible, of individual, family, and community wishes,

feeling and expectations, including family and community preferences, traditions and religious requirements relating to mourning and to funerals, and respect for individual and family privacy
- enable bereaved people, including children and young people where appropriate, to be informed and consulted during the investigation process, treating them with sensitivity, and helping them to find further help where this is necessary
- answer bereaved people's questions about coronial procedures as promptly and effectively as possible
- explain, where relevant and on request, why the coroner intends to take no further action in a particular case
- provide information about how bereaved people may appeal against or complain about the coroner's decisions and respond to appeals and complaints within the period and in the form specified by the Chief Coroner.

It is hoped that these eight objectives will significantly improve communication between the coroner's office and the bereaved and lead to an improved service.

3.2.5 When a death is reported

Paragraph 11 states that when 'a death is reported to the coroner, the coroner's office will contact the most appropriate next of kin, where known, and where possible, within one working day of the death being reported to explain why the death has been reported and what steps are likely to follow'.

Paragraph 12 sets out that the appropriate next of kin will be given information as soon as possible on where they can view the body and arrangements for viewing if they wish to do so. In addition it states that the bereaved 'will be advised sensitively if the nature of the death may cause the viewing of the body to be particularly distressing'.

3.2.6 Right of a family to report a death to the coroner

Paragraph 13 provides that if a family member believes that a doctor or other professional has not reported a death to the coroner when they should have done, then they may report a death to the coroner personally.

Paragraph 14 goes on to explain that 'the coroner will inform the family member what action he or she proposes to take when reports are made in this way'.

3.2.7 Post-mortems

Paragraph 15 sets out that where 'a coroner orders a post-mortem, the appropriate next of kin will be told by the coroner why it is necessary, when and where it will be performed and what they should do if they would like to be represented by a doctor at the post-mortem'.

Paragraph 15 also provides that if the appropriate next of kin or any other family member is unhappy with the decision to hold a post-mortem or has any queries relating to it, they should contact the coroner's office as soon as possible. It is noted however that there 'is no right of appeal to the Chief Coroner against the coroner's final decision'.

Paragraph 16 states that when coroners request additional scientific examinations on specific organs or tissues to assist with establishing the cause of death or the identity of the person who has died, the appropriate next of kin will be informed. Again, if they have any queries or questions, these should be directed to the coroner's office although again, the coroner's decision as to whether the examination should take place will be final.

Paragraph 17 sets out that in the unusual event of a second post-mortem being commissioned by coroners and the family members are dissatisfied with a coroner's reason for commissioning such an examination there will be a right of appeal to the Chief Coroner.

Paragraph 18 provides that if the coroner decides against holding a post-mortem and family members wish to challenge this decision, they should discuss this with the coroner's office and, if they remain unsatisfied, they may appeal the decision to the Chief Coroner.

Paragraph 19 states that family members 'will have a right, on request, to see reports of any post-mortems carried out although they should be aware that they may find the details distressing.'

Paragraph 20, which was inserted after the initial consultation, states that these provisions may need to be varied in respect of post-mortems resulting from criminal or suspected criminal offences. The paragraph states that the coroner's office or the Police Family Liaison Officer will discuss this with the bereaved in respect of these specific cases.

3.2.8 Keeping in touch

Paragraph 21 states that where the coroner continues his or her investigation following the post-mortem, the coroner's office will contact family members at least every three months to inform them of the status of the case, and explain the reasons for any delay.

3.2.9 Inquests

Paragraph 22 sets out that when there is to be an inquest, family members will be informed of the timing, location and the facilities available at least four weeks before the start of the inquest wherever possible.

Paragraph 23 states family members' views will be taken into account when timing the inquest. Also, information will be provided to them by the coroner's office about the inquest, for example, who is likely to be present. Information will also be provided about when legal aid may be available.

Paragraph 24 provides that if the date and/or location of the inquest must be changed, then information will be provided, wherever possible, within five working days of the decision being taken.

Paragraph 25 states that '[d]isclosure of all relevant documents to be used in an inquest will take place, on request, free of charge and in advance of an inquest, to those family members whom the coroner has determined have an interest in the investigation'. Paragraph 26 makes it clear that sometimes, for legal reasons, it will not be possible for all documents to be disclosed. However, on request, the coroner will explain the reasons for not disclosing a particular document.

Paragraph 27 provides that where the coroner takes the decision to hold 'a pre-inquest hearing, those family members known to have an interest will be informed of the time, date and location, the purpose of the hearing and their rights and opportunities during it'.

Paragraph 28 states that where possible, a private room will be provided for bereaved relatives when they attend an inquest.

Paragraph 29 informs the bereaved that some coroners now arrange for Court Support Services to operate on days when they hold inquests. The role of the support service will be to welcome the bereaved when they arrive at the inquest and explain the process. Where no such service is in place, the coroner's office will fulfil this role.

Paragraph 30 makes it clear that the media is free to report inquest proceedings, although it contains a reminder that 'there is a requirement under the Press Complaints Commission code of practice for reporting to be sensitive and sympathetic to the feelings of the bereaved'.

Paragraph 31 states that in the event of an approach by the media, the coroner's office will not release anything other than outline details of specific current cases without the consent of the appropriate next of kin. It is made clear that under no circumstances will photographs be released without the consent of the next of kin.

3.2.10 Reports to prevent future deaths

Paragraph 32 advises that at the end of an inquest, the coroner will need to decide whether the evidence heard should lead to a report being made to an organisation which may have power to take action to prevent future deaths.

Paragraph 33 states that in such cases any family members who the coroner has determined have an interest in the investigation can expect to be sent a copy of the coroner's report and any response which an organisation makes.

Paragraph 34 confirms that the coroner must send a copy of the report to the Chief Coroner who in turn will have a responsibility to provide a summary of reports made by all coroners, and any responses to them, to parliament.

3.2.11 Other rights to participation

Paragraph 35 provides that family members will be informed by the coroner, after he or she has consulted with them, of any decision to refer a death to be investigated by the coroner for a different area and the reasons for that decision. It is confirmed that the same consultation will take place if the Chief Coroner directs that investigation be carried out by a coroner from a different area. In such circumstances, the Chief Coroner has responsibility for informing family members.

Paragraph 36 makes it clear that once a body is no longer required for the coroner's purposes, coroners will not, other than in exceptional circumstances, retain the body without the consent of the family. Exceptional circumstances may include a dispute about whom the body should be released to. In cases where there is a criminal investigation, the requirement is that bodies be released for funerals within a maximum of 30 days of the death, although normally it will be much sooner than this.

Paragraph 37 reminds the bereaved that sometimes, organs or tissues are retained for additional examination. In such circumstances, the coroner should reach advance agreement with the appropriate next of kin as to what should happen to such tissues when they are no longer required for the coroner's purposes. The coroner is responsible for conveying the wishes of the next of kin to the relevant pathologist.

3.2.12 Review and appeal rights of coroners' judicial decisions

Paragraph 38 confirms that family members who have been designated by the coroner as 'interested persons' will have the right to appeal the following decisions:

- if the coroner decides there will NOT be a post-mortem or that there will be a second post-mortem of the same type as previously requested
- whether there will be an investigation by the coroner
- whether to resume an investigation suspended by the coroner
- whether an inquest should be held with a jury.

Paragraph 39 provides that in addition to the above the appropriate next of kin may make representations to the Chief Coroner if dissatisfied where, in exceptional circumstances, the coroner proposes to retain the body of the person who has died for more than 30 days after the death.

Paragraph 40 states that in most cases, if there is disagreement between the coroner and the family member about any of the above, it is likely be resolved through discussion. If for whatever reason this is not possible, the family member can appeal to the Chief Coroner setting out clearly the grounds for appealing the decision, wherever possible, within a maximum of 15 working days (one working day if it concerns a post-mortem) of the decision being taken.

Paragraph 41 confirms that in addition, appeals will also be possible against decisions in relation to:

- the coroner discontinuing an investigation before an inquest;

- the decision given at the end of an inquest.

Presumably, the decision given at the end of an inquest means the verdict. However, other decisions are made at the end of an inquest, e.g. whether to issue a Rule 43 letter.

Paragraph 42 states that the family will be allowed 60 working days to lodge their appeal in the instances outlined in paragraphs 38–41, 'although consideration will be given as to whether appeals can be heard beyond this time limit'.

Paragraph 43 states that most appeals are likely to be decided on the papers. However, in any case where the Chief Coroner decides that an oral hearing is required, it is likely that additional time will be needed to give any judgment. It is stated that the family will be kept informed by the Chief Coroner's office of the likely timescale.

Paragraph 44 provides that the Chief Coroner's office will inform the person who has appealed (and others interested in the appeal) of the outcome.

3.2.13 Deaths abroad

Paragraph 45 advises that coroners will investigate deaths abroad where the apparent circumstances would have led them to have done so had the death occurred in England or Wales. This paragraph makes it clear that in such circumstances, the standards of service outlined in this charter may need to be varied.

3.2.14 Responsibilities of family members

Paragraphs 46 to 49 inclusive deal with the responsibilities of family members. All these paragraphs were inserted after the initial consultation.

Paragraph 46 states that '[f]amily members of the person who has died have a responsibility to provide all information to the coroner's office that is relevant to the investigation'.

Paragraph 47 provides that family members should treat any information or documents they have disclosed to them with confidence if requested to do so.

Paragraph 48 advises that family members should inform the coroner's office of any change to details, such as their address, to ensure that they can be contacted promptly.

Paragraph 49 requests that family members treat the coroner and his staff with courtesy and respect at all stages of the investigation.

3.2.15 Disability issues

Paragraph 50 provides that coroners will provide appropriate access to coroners' courts and offices as far as practicable and taking account of statutory responsibilities. Reasonable adjustments will be made, wherever possible, to meet the needs of those with disabilities.

3.2.16 Availability of support and bereavement services

Paragraph 51 states that with the assistance of the Chief Coroner, coroners will hold information on the main local and national voluntary bodies, support groups and faith groups which can offer help or support to bereaved people, including when bereavement is as a result of particular types of incidents or circumstances. They will make this information available to family members or the representatives unless otherwise requested.

3.2.17 Monitoring service standards

Paragraphs 52 and 53 deal with the monitoring of service standards. Their aims are to improve service standards and to try to establish consistency between coroners' areas which was a major cause of concern in the early stages of the Bill.

Paragraph 52 states that the Chief Coroner will require coroners to provide regular reports on their performance against national standards. Further to this the Chief Coroner will then give the Lord Chancellor an annual report which will include an assessment of the consistency of standards across coroners' areas.

Paragraph 53 confirms that independent inspections of the service will be carried out and will include as part of the inspection, consultation with bereaved people. It is stated that 'In addition, the Chief Coroner may arrange surveys of service users from time to time'.

3.2.18 Other complaints and feedback

Paragraph 54 provides that bereaved people wishing to make a complaint about a failure to deliver in relation to this charter should do so in the first instance to the coroner. If they are not satisfied with the response then they should elevate their complaint to the Chief Coroner.

Paragraph 55 confirms that '[c]oroners are committed to providing a service which meets the needs of bereaved people at a sensitive time, and welcomes general feedback from bereaved people about their experiences, including feedback on where the service has performed well'. Feedback should be directed to the coroner who dealt with the case or the Chief Coroner.

3.2.19 Other responsibilities of the Chief Coroner

Paragraph 56 states that the Chief Coroner 'will be responsible for setting national minimum standards across a range of coroner functions'. In relation to the services for bereaved families, this could include standards in relation to particular types of death or suspected deaths, e.g. military deaths or deaths apparently resulting from suicide.

Paragraph 57 confirms that this is only a draft charter and as such it is intended as a guide to the kind of service it is envisaged will be provided in the reformed system.

3.3 CONCLUSION

The draft charter has laudable aims and many coronial areas are already operating to these good standards. The fact that there is a need for such a charter highlights the fact that we will still have a fragmented coronial service. Sadly, the Act has failed to make the coronial service a national one thereby making inconsistent service an inevitability.

The biggest concern with the charter, as with the Act, is funding.

Will there be funding to pay for this improved level of service? Many critics fear not. In particular, there is concern that as the coronial service will still be funded locally, the quality in relation to service delivery will vary. This is unfortunate.

Funding is relevant not only in relation to how the coronial service engages with the bereaved, but in relation to how the bereaved can participate in the process, including attending and contributing at inquests. Many argue that public funding should be more widely available if arguments of lack of engagement are to be truly rebutted.

As with the Act itself, the question of how the Chief Coroner will be able to enforce compliance and consistency when the service is locally funded is yet to be answered.

So, like anything intended to improve the service for the bereaved, the charter is to be welcomed. However, its success is far from guaranteed.

Appendix 1
CORONERS AND JUSTICE ACT 2009 (EXTRACTS)

2009 CHAPTER 25

An Act to amend the law relating to coroners, to investigation of deaths and to certification and registration of deaths; to amend the criminal law; to make provision about criminal justice and about dealing with offenders; to make provision about the Commissioner for Victims and Witnesses; to make provision relating to the security of court and other buildings; to make provision about legal aid and about payments for legal services provided in connection with employment matters; to make provision for payments to be made by offenders in respect of benefits derived from the exploitation of material pertaining to offences; to amend the Data Protection Act 1998; and for connected purposes. [12th November 2009]

BE IT ENACTED by the Queen's most Excellent Majesty, by and with the advice and consent of the Lords Spiritual and Temporal, and Commons, in this present Parliament assembled, and by the authority of the same, as follows: –

PART 1 CORONERS ETC

CHAPTER 1 INVESTIGATIONS INTO DEATHS

Duty to investigate

1 Duty to investigate certain deaths

(1) A senior coroner who is made aware that the body of a deceased person is within that coroner's area must as soon as practicable conduct an investigation into the person's death if subsection (2) applies.

(2) This subsection applies if the coroner has reason to suspect that –

(a) the deceased died a violent or unnatural death,
(b) the cause of death is unknown, or
(c) the deceased died while in custody or otherwise in state detention.

(3) Subsection (1) is subject to sections 2 to 4.

(4) A senior coroner who has reason to believe that –

(a) a death has occurred in or near the coroner's area,
(b) the circumstances of the death are such that there should be an investigation into it, and
(c) the duty to conduct an investigation into the death under subsection (1) does not arise because of the destruction, loss or absence of the body,

may report the matter to the Chief Coroner.

(5) On receiving a report under subsection (4) the Chief Coroner may direct a senior

coroner (who does not have to be the one who made the report) to conduct an investigation into the death.

(6) The coroner to whom a direction is given under subsection (5) must conduct an investigation into the death as soon as practicable. This is subject to section 3.

(7) A senior coroner may make whatever enquiries seem necessary in order to decide –

(a) whether the duty under subsection (1) arises;
(b) whether the power under subsection (4) arises.

(8) This Chapter is subject to Schedule 10.

Investigation by other coroner

2 Request for other coroner to conduct investigation

(1) A senior coroner (coroner A) who is under a duty under section 1(1) to conduct an investigation into a person's death may request a senior coroner for another area (coroner B) to conduct the investigation.

(2) If coroner B agrees to conduct the investigation, that coroner (and not coroner A) must conduct the investigation, and must do so as soon as practicable.

(3) Subsection (2) does not apply if a direction concerning the investigation is given under section 3 before coroner B agrees to conduct the investigation.

(4) Subsection (2) is subject to –

(a) any direction concerning the investigation that is given under section 3 after the agreement, and
(b) section 4.

(5) A senior coroner must give to the Chief Coroner notice in writing of any request made by him or her under subsection (1), stating whether or not the other coroner agreed to it.

3 Direction for other coroner to conduct investigation

(1) The Chief Coroner may direct a senior coroner (coroner B) to conduct an investigation under this Part into a person's death even though, apart from the direction, a different senior coroner (coroner A) would be under a duty to conduct it.

(2) Where a direction is given under this section, coroner B (and not coroner A) must conduct the investigation, and must do so as soon as practicable.

(3) Subsection (2) is subject to –

(a) any subsequent direction concerning the investigation that is given under this section, and
(b) section 4.

(4) The Chief Coroner must give notice in writing of a direction under this section to coroner A.

(5) A reference in this section to conducting an investigation, in the case of an investigation that has already begun, is to be read as a reference to continuing to conduct the investigation.

Discontinuance of investigation

4 Discontinuance where cause of death revealed by post-mortem examination

(1) A senior coroner who is responsible for conducting an investigation under this Part into a person's death must discontinue the investigation if –

(a) an examination under section 14 reveals the cause of death before the coroner has begun holding an inquest into the death, and
(b) the coroner thinks that it is not necessary to continue the investigation.

(2) Subsection (1) does not apply if the coroner has reason to suspect that the deceased –

(a) died a violent or unnatural death, or
(b) died while in custody or otherwise in state detention.

(3) Where a senior coroner discontinues an investigation into a death under this section –

(a) the coroner may not hold an inquest into the death;
(b) no determination or finding under section 10(1) may be made in respect of the death.

This subsection does not prevent a fresh investigation under this Part from being conducted into the death.

(4) A senior coroner who discontinues an investigation into a death under this section must, if requested to do so in writing by an interested person, give to that person as soon as practicable a written explanation as to why the investigation was discontinued.

Purpose of investigation

5 Matters to be ascertained

(1) The purpose of an investigation under this Part into a person's death is to ascertain –

(a) who the deceased was;
(b) how, when and where the deceased came by his or her death;
(c) the particulars (if any) required by the 1953 Act to be registered concerning the death.

(2) Where necessary in order to avoid a breach of any Convention rights (within the meaning of the Human Rights Act 1998), the purpose mentioned in subsection (1)(b) is to be read as including the purpose of ascertaining in what circumstances the deceased came by his or her death.

(3) Neither the senior coroner conducting an investigation under this Part into a person's death nor the jury (if there is one) may express any opinion on any matter other than –

(a) the questions mentioned in subsection (1)(a) and (b) (read with subsection (2) where applicable);
(b) the particulars mentioned in subsection (1)(c).

This is subject to paragraph 7 of Schedule 5.

Inquests

6 Duty to hold inquest

A senior coroner who conducts an investigation under this Part into a person's death must (as part of the investigation) hold an inquest into the death.

This is subject to section 4(3)(a).

7 Whether jury required

(1) An inquest into a death must be held without a jury unless subsection (2) or (3) applies.

(2) An inquest into a death must be held with a jury if the senior coroner has reason to suspect –

(a) that the deceased died while in custody or otherwise in state detention, and that either –

(i) the death was a violent or unnatural one, or
(ii) the cause of death is unknown,

(b) that the death resulted from an act or omission of –

(i) a police officer, or
(ii) a member of a service police force,

in the purported execution of the officer's or member's duty as such, or

(c) that the death was caused by a notifiable accident, poisoning or disease.

(3) An inquest into a death may be held with a jury if the senior coroner thinks that there is sufficient reason for doing so.

(4) For the purposes of subsection (2)(c) an accident, poisoning or disease is 'notifiable' if notice of it is required under any Act to be given –

(a) to a government department,
(b) to an inspector or other officer of a government department, or
(c) to an inspector appointed under section 19 of the Health and Safety at Work etc. Act 1974.

8 Assembling a jury

(1) The jury at an inquest (where there is a jury) is to consist of seven, eight, nine, ten or eleven persons.

(2) For the purpose of summoning a jury, a senior coroner may summon persons (whether within or without the coroner area for which that coroner is appointed) to attend at the time and place stated in the summons.

(3) Once assembled, the members of a jury are to be sworn by or before the coroner to inquire into the death of the deceased and to give a true determination according to the evidence.

(4) Only a person who is qualified to serve as a juror in the Crown Court, the High Court and the county courts, under section 1 of the Juries Act 1974, is qualified to serve as a juror at an inquest.

(5) The senior coroner may put to a person summoned under this section any questions that appear necessary to establish whether or not the person is qualified to serve as a juror at an inquest.

9 Determinations and findings by jury

(1) Subject to subsection (2), a determination or finding that a jury is required to make under section 10(1) must be unanimous.

(2) A determination or finding need not be unanimous if –

(a) only one or two of the jury do not agree on it, and
(b) the jury has deliberated for a period of time that the senior coroner thinks reasonable in view of the nature and complexity of the case.

Before accepting a determination or finding not agreed on by all the members of the jury, the coroner must require one of them to announce publicly how many agreed and how many did not.

(3) If the members of the jury, or the number of members required by subsection (2)(a), do not agree on a determination or finding, the coroner may discharge the jury and another one may be summoned in its place.

Outcome of investigation

10 Determinations and findings to be made

(1) After hearing the evidence at an inquest into a death, the senior coroner (if there is no jury) or the jury (if there is one) must –

(a) make a determination as to the questions mentioned in section 5(1)(a) and (b) (read with section 5(2) where applicable), and

(b) if particulars are required by the 1953 Act to be registered concerning the death, make a finding as to those particulars.

(2) A determination under subsection (1)(a) may not be framed in such a way as to appear to determine any question of –

(a) criminal liability on the part of a named person, or
(b) civil liability.

(3) In subsection (2) 'criminal liability' includes liability in respect of a service offence.

Suspension

11 Duty or power to suspend or resume investigations

Schedule 1 makes provision about suspension and resumption of investigations.

Death of service personnel abroad

12 Investigation in Scotland

(1) This section applies to the death outside the United Kingdom of a person within subsection (2) or (3).

(2) A person is within this subsection if at the time of the death the person was subject to service law by virtue of section 367 of the Armed Forces Act 2006 and was engaged in –

(a) active service,
(b) activities carried on in preparation for, or directly in support of, active service, or
(c) training carried out in order to improve or maintain the effectiveness of those engaged in active service.

(3) A person is within this subsection if at the time of the death the person was not subject to service law but –

(a) by virtue of paragraph 7 of Schedule 15 to the Armed Forces Act 2006 was a civilian subject to service discipline, and
(b) was accompanying persons subject to service law who were engaged in active service.

(4) If –

(a) the person's body is within Scotland or is expected to be brought to the United Kingdom, and
(b) the Secretary of State thinks that it may be appropriate for the circumstances of the death to be investigated under the Fatal Accidents and Sudden Deaths Inquiry (Scotland) Act 1976,

the Secretary of State may notify the Lord Advocate accordingly.

(5) If –

(a) the person's body is within England and Wales, and
(b) the Chief Coroner thinks that it may be appropriate for the circumstances of the death to be investigated under that Act,

the Chief Coroner may notify the Lord Advocate accordingly.

13 Investigation in England and Wales despite body being brought to Scotland

(1) The Chief Coroner may direct a senior coroner to conduct an investigation into a person's death if –

(a) the deceased is a person within subsection (2) or (3) of section 12,

(b) the Lord Advocate has been notified under subsection (4) or (5) of that section in relation to the death,
(c) the body of the deceased has been brought to Scotland,
(d) no inquiry into the circumstances of the death under the Fatal Accidents and Sudden Deaths Inquiry (Scotland) Act 1976 has been held (or any such inquiry that has been started has not been concluded),
(e) the Lord Advocate notifies the Chief Coroner that, in the Lord Advocate's view, it may be appropriate for an investigation under this Part into the death to be conducted, and
(f) the Chief Coroner has reason to suspect that –
    (i) the deceased died a violent or unnatural death,
    (ii) the cause of death is unknown, or
    (iii) the deceased died while in custody or otherwise in state detention.

(2) The coroner to whom a direction is given under subsection (1) must conduct an investigation into the death as soon as practicable.

This is subject to section 3.

Ancillary powers of coroners in relation to deaths

14 Post-mortem examinations

(1) A senior coroner may request a suitable practitioner to make a post-mortem examination of a body if –

(a) the coroner is responsible for conducting an investigation under this Part into the death of the person in question, or
(b) a post-mortem examination is necessary to enable the coroner to decide whether the death is one into which the coroner has a duty under section 1(1) to conduct an investigation.

(2) A request under subsection (1) may specify the kind of examination to be made.
(3) For the purposes of subsection (1) a person is a suitable practitioner if he or she –

(a) is a registered medical practitioner, or
(b) in a case where a particular kind of examination is requested, a practitioner of a description designated by the Chief Coroner as suitable to make examinations of that kind.

(4) Where a person informs the senior coroner that, in the informant's opinion, death was caused wholly or partly by the improper or negligent treatment of a registered medical practitioner or other person, that practitioner or other person –

(a) must not make, or assist at, an examination under this section of the body, but
(b) is entitled to be represented at such an examination.

This subsection has no effect as regards a post-mortem examination already made.

(5) A person who makes a post-mortem examination under this section must as soon as practicable report the result of the examination to the senior coroner in whatever form the coroner requires.

15 Power to remove body

(1) A senior coroner who –

(a) is responsible for conducting an investigation under this Part into a person's death, or
(b) needs to request a post-mortem examination under section 14 in order to

decide whether the death is one into which the coroner has a duty under section 1(1) to conduct an investigation,

may order the body to be removed to any suitable place.

(2) That place may be within the coroner's area or elsewhere.

(3) The senior coroner may not order the removal of a body under this section to a place provided by a person who has not consented to its being removed there.

This does not apply to a place within the coroner's area that is provided by a district council, a county council, a county borough council, a London borough council or the Common Council.

Miscellaneous

16 Investigations lasting more than a year

(1) A senior coroner who is conducting an investigation under this Part into a person's death that has not been completed or discontinued within a year –

- (a) must notify the Chief Coroner of that fact;
- (b) must notify the Chief Coroner of the date on which the investigation is completed or discontinued.

(2) In subsection (1) 'within a year' means within the period of 12 months beginning with the day on which the coroner was made aware that the person's body was within the coroner's area.

(3) The Chief Coroner must keep a register of notifications given under subsection (1).

17 Monitoring of and training for investigations into deaths of service personnel

(1) The Chief Coroner must –

- (a) monitor investigations under this Part into service deaths;
- (b) secure that coroners conducting such investigations are suitably trained to do so.

(2) In this section 'service death' means the death of a person who at the time of the death was subject to service law by virtue of section 367 of the Armed Forces Act 2006 and was engaged in –

- (a) active service,
- (b) activities carried on in preparation for, or directly in support of, active service, or
- (c) training carried out in order to improve or maintain the effectiveness of those engaged in active service.

CHAPTER 2 NOTIFICATION, CERTIFICATION AND REGISTRATION OF DEATHS

18 Notification by medical practitioner to senior coroner

(1) The Lord Chancellor may make regulations requiring a registered medical practitioner, in prescribed cases or circumstances, to notify a senior coroner of a death of which the practitioner is aware.

(2) Before making regulations under this section the Lord Chancellor must consult –

- (a) the Secretary of State for Health, and
- (b) the Chief Coroner.

19 Medical examiners

(1) Primary Care Trusts (in England) and Local Health Boards (in Wales) must appoint persons as medical examiners to discharge the functions conferred on medical examiners by or under this Chapter.
(2) Each Trust or Board must –

(a) appoint enough medical examiners, and make available enough funds and other resources, to enable those functions to be discharged in its area;
(b) monitor the performance of medical examiners appointed by the Trust or Board by reference to any standards or levels of performance that those examiners are expected to attain.

(3) A person may be appointed as a medical examiner only if, at the time of the appointment, he or she –

(a) is a registered medical practitioner and has been throughout the previous 5 years, and
(b) practises as such or has done within the previous 5 years.

(4) The appropriate Minister may by regulations make –

(a) provision about the terms of appointment of medical examiners and about termination of appointment;
(b) provision for the payment to medical examiners of remuneration, expenses, fees, compensation for termination of appointment, pensions, allowances or gratuities;
(c) provision as to training –

(i) to be undertaken as a precondition for appointment as a medical examiner;
(ii) to be undertaken by medical examiners;

(d) provision about the procedure to be followed in connection with the exercise of functions by medical examiners;
(e) provision conferring functions on medical examiners;
(f) provision for functions of medical examiners to be exercised, during a period of emergency, by persons not meeting the criteria in subsection (3).

(5) Nothing in this section, or in regulations under this section, gives a Primary Care Trust or a Local Health Board any role in relation to the way in which medical examiners exercise their professional judgment as medical practitioners.
(6) In this section 'the appropriate Minister' means –

(a) in relation to England, the Secretary of State;
(b) in relation to Wales, the Welsh Ministers.

(7) For the purposes of this section a 'period of emergency' is a period certified as such by the Secretary of State on the basis that there is or has been, or is about to be, an event or situation involving or causing, or having the potential to cause, a substantial loss of human life throughout, or in any part of, England and Wales.
(8) A certification under subsection (7) must specify –

(a) the date when the period of emergency begins, and
(b) the date when it is to end.

(9) Subsection (8)(b) does not prevent the Secretary of State certifying a new period of emergency in respect of the same event or situation.

20 Medical certificate of cause of death

(1) The Secretary of State may by regulations make the following provision in relation to a death that is required to be registered under Part 2 of the 1953 Act –

(a) provision requiring a registered medical practitioner who attended the deceased before his or her death (an 'attending practitioner') –

(i) to prepare a certificate stating the cause of death to the best of the practitioner's knowledge and belief (an 'attending practitioner's certificate'), or
(ii) where the practitioner is unable to establish the cause of death, to refer the case to a senior coroner;

(b) provision requiring a copy of an attending practitioner's certificate to be given to a medical examiner;
(c) provision allowing an attending practitioner, if invited to do so by the medical examiner or a registrar, to issue a fresh attending practitioner's certificate superseding the existing one;
(d) provision requiring a senior coroner to refer a case to a medical examiner;
(e) provision requiring a medical examiner to make whatever enquiries appear to be necessary in order to confirm or establish the cause of death;
(f) provision requiring a medical examiner to whom a copy of an attending practitioner's certificate has been given –

(i) to confirm the cause of death stated on the certificate and to notify a registrar that the cause of death has been confirmed, or
(ii) where the examiner is unable to confirm the cause of death, to refer the case to a senior coroner;

(g) provision for an attending practitioner's certificate, once the cause of death has been confirmed as mentioned in paragraph (f), to be given to a registrar;
(h) provision requiring a medical examiner to whom a case has been referred by a senior coroner –

(i) to issue a certificate stating the cause of death to the best of the examiner's knowledge and belief (a 'medical examiner's certificate') and to notify a registrar that the certificate has been issued, or
(ii) where the examiner is unable to establish the cause of the death, to refer the case back to the coroner;

(i) provision for a medical examiner's certificate to be given to a registrar;
(j) provision allowing a medical examiner, if invited to do so by the registrar, to issue a fresh medical examiner's certificate superseding the existing one;
(k) provision requiring a medical examiner or someone acting on behalf of a medical examiner –

(i) to discuss the cause of death with the informant or with some other person whom the examiner considers appropriate, and
(ii) to give him or her the opportunity to mention any matter that might cause a senior coroner to think that the death should be investigated under section 1;

(l) provision for confirmation to be given in writing, either by the informant or by a person of a prescribed description, that the requirement referred to in paragraph (k) has been complied with;
(m) provision prescribing forms (including the form of an attending practitioner's certificate and of a medical examiner's certificate) for use by persons exercising functions under the regulations, and requiring the forms to be made available to those persons;
(n) provision requiring the Chief Medical Officer of the Department of Health, after consulting –

(i) the Officer with corresponding functions in relation to Wales,
(ii) the Registrar General, and

(iii) the Statistics Board,

to issue guidance as to how certificates and other forms under the regulations are to be completed;

(o) provision for certificates or other forms under the regulations to be signed or otherwise authenticated.

(2) Regulations under subsection (1) imposing a requirement –

(a) may prescribe a period within which the requirement is to be complied with;
(b) may prescribe cases or circumstances in which the requirement does, or does not, apply (and may, in particular, provide for the requirement not to apply during a period of emergency).

(3) The power under subsection (1)(m) to prescribe forms is exercisable only after consultation with –

(a) the Welsh Ministers,
(b) the Registrar General, and
(c) the Statistics Board.

(4) Regulations under subsection (1) may provide for functions that would otherwise be exercisable by a registered medical practitioner who attended the deceased before his or her death to be exercisable, during a period of emergency, by a registered medical practitioner who did not do so.
(5) The appropriate Minister may by regulations provide for a fee to be payable to a Primary Care Trust or Local Health Board in respect of –

(a) a medical examiner's confirmation of the cause of death stated on an attending practitioner's certificate, or
(b) the issue of a medical examiner's certificate.

(6) Section 7 of the Cremation Act 1902 (regulations as to burning) does not require the Secretary of State to make regulations, or to include any provision in regulations, if or to the extent that he or she thinks it unnecessary to do so in consequence of –

(a) provision made by regulations under this Chapter or by Coroners regulations, or
(b) provision contained in, or made by regulations under, Part 2 of the 1953 Act as amended by Part 1 of Schedule 21 to this Act.

(7) In this section –

'the appropriate Minister' has the same meaning as in section 19;

'informant', in relation to a death, means the person who gave particulars concerning the death to the registrar under section 16 or 17 of the 1953 Act;

'period of emergency' has the same meaning as in section 19;

'the Statistics Board' means the body corporate established by section 1 of the Statistics and Registration Service Act 2007.

21 National Medical Examiner

(1) The Secretary of State may appoint a person as National Medical Examiner.
(2) The National Medical Examiner is to have –

(a) the function of issuing guidance to medical examiners with a view to securing that they carry out their functions in an effective and proportionate manner;
(b) any further functions conferred by regulations made by the Secretary of State.

(3) Before appointing a person as National Medical Examiner or making regulations under subsection (2)(b), the Secretary of State must consult the Welsh Ministers.

(4) A person may be appointed as National Medical Examiner only if, at the time of the appointment, he or she –

(a) is a registered medical practitioner and has been throughout the previous 5 years, and

(b) practises as such or has done within the previous 5 years.

(5) The appointment of a person as National Medical Examiner is to be on whatever terms and conditions the Secretary of State thinks appropriate.

(6) The Secretary of State may pay to the National Medical Examiner –

(a) amounts determined by the Secretary of State by way of remuneration or allowances;

(b) amounts determined by the Secretary of State towards expenses incurred in performing functions as such.

(7) The National Medical Examiner may amend or revoke any guidance issued under subsection (2)(a).

(8) The National Medical Examiner must consult the Welsh Ministers before issuing, amending or revoking any such guidance.

(9) Medical examiners must have regard to any such guidance in carrying out their functions.

CHAPTER 3 CORONER AREAS, APPOINTMENTS ETC

22 Coroner areas

Schedule 2 makes provision about coroner areas.

23 Appointment etc of senior coroners, area coroners and assistant coroners

Schedule 3 makes provision about the appointment etc of senior coroners, area coroners and assistant coroners.

24 Provision of staff and accommodation

(1) The relevant authority for a coroner area –

(a) must secure the provision of whatever officers and other staff are needed by the coroners for that area to carry out their functions;

(b) must provide, or secure the provision of, accommodation that is appropriate to the needs of those coroners in carrying out their functions;

(c) must maintain, or secure the maintenance of, accommodation provided under paragraph (b).

(2) Subsection (1)(a) applies to a particular coroner area only if, or to the extent that, the necessary officers and other staff for that area are not provided by a police authority.

(3) Subsection (1)(c) does not apply in relation to accommodation the maintenance of which is the responsibility of a person other than the relevant authority in question.

(4) In deciding how to discharge its duties under subsection (1)(b) and (c), the relevant authority for a coroner area must take into account the views of the senior coroner for that area.

(5) A reference in subsection (1) to the coroners for an area is to the senior coroner, and any area coroners or assistant coroners, for that area.

CHAPTER 4 INVESTIGATIONS CONCERNING TREASURE

25 Coroner for Treasure and Assistant Coroners for Treasure

Schedule 4 makes provision about the appointment etc of the Coroner for Treasure and Assistant Coroners for Treasure.

26 Investigations concerning treasure

(1) The Coroner for Treasure must conduct an investigation concerning an object in respect of which notification is given under section 8(1) of the Treasure Act 1996.
(2) The Coroner for Treasure may conduct an investigation concerning an object in respect of which notification has not been given under that section if he or she has reason to suspect that the object is treasure.
(3) The Coroner for Treasure may conduct an investigation concerning an object if he or she has reason to suspect that the object is treasure trove.
(4) Subsections (1) to (3) are subject to section 29.
(5) The purpose of an investigation under this section is to ascertain –

(a) whether or not the object in question is treasure or treasure trove;
(b) if it is treasure or treasure trove, who found it, where it was found and when it was found.

(6) Senior coroners, area coroners and assistant coroners have no functions in relation to objects that are or may be treasure or treasure trove. This is subject to paragraph 11 of Schedule 4 (which enables an assistant coroner acting as an Assistant Coroner for Treasure to perform functions of the Coroner for Treasure).

27 Inquests concerning treasure

(1) The Coroner for Treasure may, as part of an investigation under section 26, hold an inquest concerning the object in question (a 'treasure inquest').
(2) A treasure inquest must be held without a jury, unless the Coroner for Treasure thinks there is sufficient reason for it to be held with a jury.
(3) In relation to a treasure inquest held with a jury, sections 8 and 9 apply with the following modifications –

(a) a reference to a senior coroner is to be read as a reference to the Coroner for Treasure;
(b) the reference in section 8(3) to the death of the deceased is to be read as a reference to the matters mentioned in section 26(5).

28 Outcome of investigations concerning treasure

Where the Coroner for Treasure has conducted an investigation under section 26, a determination as to the question mentioned in subsection (5)(a) of that section, and (where applicable) the questions mentioned in subsection (5)(b) of that section, must be made –

(a) by the Coroner for Treasure after considering the evidence (where an inquest is not held),
(b) by the Coroner for Treasure after hearing the evidence (where an inquest is held without a jury), or
(c) by the jury after hearing the evidence (where an inquest is held with a jury).

29 Exception to duty to investigate

(1) Where the Coroner for Treasure is conducting, or proposes to conduct, an investigation under section 26 concerning –

(a) an object that would vest in the Crown under the Treasure Act 1996 if the object was in fact treasure and there were no prior interests or rights, or
(b) an object that would belong to the Crown under the law relating to treasure trove if the object was in fact treasure trove,

the Secretary of State may give notice to the Coroner for Treasure disclaiming, on behalf of the Crown, any title that the Crown may have to the object.

(2) Where the Coroner for Treasure is conducting, or proposes to conduct, an investigation under section 26 concerning –

(a) an object that would vest in the franchisee under the Treasure Act 1996 if the object was in fact treasure and there were no prior interests or rights, or
(b) an object that would belong to the franchisee under the law relating to treasure trove if the object was in fact treasure trove,

the franchisee may give notice to the Coroner for Treasure disclaiming any title that the franchisee may have to the object.

(3) A notice under subsection (1) or (2) may be given only before the making of a determination under section 28.
(4) Where a notice is given under subsection (1) or (2) –

(a) the object is to be treated as not vesting in or belonging to the Crown, or (as the case may be) the franchisee, under the Treasure Act 1996, or the law relating to treasure trove;
(b) the Coroner for Treasure may not conduct an investigation concerning the object under section 26 or, if an investigation has already begun, may not continue with it;
(c) without prejudice to the interests or rights of others, the object may be delivered to a person in accordance with a code of practice published under section 11 of the Treasure Act 1996.

(5) For the purposes of this section the franchisee, in relation to an object, is the person who –

(a) was, immediately before the commencement of section 4 of the Treasure Act 1996, or
(b) apart from that Act, as successor in title, would have been,

the franchisee of the Crown in right of treasure trove for the place where the object was found.

30 Duty to notify Coroner for Treasure etc of acquisition of certain objects

(1) After section 8 of the Treasure Act 1996 there is inserted –

'8A Duty to notify coroner of acquisition of certain objects

(1) A person who –

(a) acquires property in an object, and
(b) believes or has reasonable grounds for believing –

(i) that the object is treasure, and
(ii) that notification in respect of the object has not been given under section 8(1) or this subsection,

must notify the Coroner for Treasure before the end of the notice period.

(2) The notice period is fourteen days beginning with –

(a) the day after the person acquires property in the object; or
(b) if later, the day on which the person first believes or has reason to believe –

(i) that the object is treasure; and
(ii) that notification in respect of the object has not been given under section 8(1) or subsection (1) of this section.

(3) Any person who fails to comply with subsection (1) is guilty of an offence if –

(a) notification in respect of the object has not been given under section 8(1) or subsection (1) of this section; and
(b) there has been no investigation in relation to the object.

(4) Any person guilty of an offence under this section is liable on summary conviction to –

(a) imprisonment for a term not exceeding 51 weeks;
(b) a fine of an amount not exceeding level 5 on the standard scale; or
(c) both.

(5) In proceedings for an offence under this section, it is a defence for the defendant to show that he had, and has continued to have, a reasonable excuse for failing to notify the Coroner for Treasure.
(6) If the office of Coroner for Treasure is vacant, notification under subsection (1) must be given to an Assistant Coroner for Treasure.
(7) In determining for the purposes of this section whether a person has acquired property in an object, section 4 is to be disregarded.
(8) For the purposes of an investigation in relation to an object in respect of which notification has been given under subsection (1), the object is to be presumed, in the absence of evidence to the contrary, to have been found in England and Wales after the commencement of section 4.
(9) This section has effect subject to section 8B.
(10) In this section 'investigation' means an investigation under section 26 of the Coroners and Justice Act 2009.
(11) In its application to Northern Ireland this section has effect as if –

(a) in subsection (1), for "Coroner for Treasure" there were substituted "coroner for the district in which the object is located";
(b) in subsection (3)(b), for "investigation" there were substituted "inquest";
(c) in subsection (4)(a), for "51 weeks" there were substituted "three months";
(d) in subsection (5), for "Coroner for Treasure" there were substituted "coroner";
(e) in subsection (6), for the words from "Coroner for Treasure" to "Assistant Coroner for Treasure" there were substituted "coroner for a district is vacant, the person acting as coroner for that district is the coroner for the purposes of subsection (1)";
(f) in subsection (8), for "investigation" there were substituted "inquest" and for "England and Wales" there were substituted "Northern Ireland";
(g) in subsection (10), for ""investigation" means an investigation under section 26 of the Coroners and Justice Act 2009" there were substituted ""inquest" means an inquest held under section 7".'

(2) In section 10 of that Act (rewards), in subsection (5) (persons to whom reward may be paid), at the end insert –

'(d) any person who gave notice under section 8A in respect of the treasure.'

(3) In relation to an offence under section 8A of that Act (inserted by subsection (1) above) committed before the commencement of section 280(2) of the Criminal Justice Act 2003, a reference in the inserted section to 51 weeks is to be read as a reference to three months.

31 Code of practice under the Treasure Act 1996

(1) A code of practice under section 11 of the Treasure Act 1996 may make provision to do with objects in respect of which notice is given under section 29(1) or (2).

(2) No civil liability on the part of the Coroner for Treasure arises where he or she delivers an object, or takes any other action, in accordance with a code of practice under section 11 of the Treasure Act 1996.

CHAPTER 5 FURTHER PROVISION TO DO WITH INVESTIGATIONS AND DEATHS

32 Powers of coroners

Schedule 5 makes provision about powers of senior coroners and the Coroner for Treasure.

33 Offences

Schedule 6 makes provision about offences relating to jurors, witnesses and evidence.

34 Allowances, fees and expenses

Schedule 7 makes provision about allowances, fees and expenses.

CHAPTER 6 GOVERNANCE ETC

35 Chief Coroner and Deputy Chief Coroners

(1) Schedule 8 makes provision about the appointment etc of the Chief Coroner and Deputy Chief Coroners.
(2) The Lord Chief Justice may nominate a judicial office holder (as defined in section 109(4) of the Constitutional Reform Act 2005) to exercise any of the functions of the Lord Chief Justice under Schedule 8.

36 Reports and advice to the Lord Chancellor from the Chief Coroner

(1) The Chief Coroner must give the Lord Chancellor a report for each calendar year.
(2) The report must cover –

(a) matters that the Chief Coroner wishes to bring to the attention of the Lord Chancellor;
(b) matters that the Lord Chancellor has asked the Chief Coroner to cover in the report.

(3) The report must contain an assessment for the year of the consistency of standards between coroners areas.
(4) The report must also contain a summary for the year of –

(a) the number and length of –

(i) investigations in respect of which notification was given under subsection (1)(a) or (b) of section 16, and
(ii) investigations that were not concluded or discontinued by the end of the year and in respect of which notification was given under subsection (1)(a) of that section in a previous year,

as well as the reasons for the length of those investigations and the measures taken with a view to keeping them from being unnecessarily lengthy;

(b) the number, nature and outcome of appeals under section 40(1), (3), (4), (5) or (9);
(c) the matters recorded under paragraph 4 of Schedule 5;
(d) the matters reported under paragraph 7 of that Schedule and the responses given under sub-paragraph (2) of that paragraph.

(5) A report for a year under this section must be given to the Lord Chancellor by 1 July in the following year.
(6) The Lord Chancellor must publish each report given under this section and must lay a copy of it before each House of Parliament.
(7) If requested to do so by the Lord Chancellor, the Chief Coroner must give advice to the Lord Chancellor about particular matters relating to the operation of the coroner system.

37 Regulations about training

(1) The Chief Coroner may, with the agreement of the Lord Chancellor, make regulations about the training of –

(a) senior coroners, area coroners and assistant coroners;
(b) the Coroner for Treasure and Assistant Coroners for Treasure;
(c) coroners' officers and other staff assisting persons within paragraph (a) or (b).

(2) The regulations may (in particular) make provision as to –

(a) the kind of training to be undertaken;
(b) the amount of training to be undertaken;
(c) the frequency with which it is to be undertaken.

38 Medical Adviser and Deputy Medical Advisers to the Chief Coroner

Schedule 9 makes provision about the appointment etc of the Medical Adviser to the Chief Coroner and Deputy Medical Advisers to the Chief Coroner.

39 Inspection of coroner system

(1) It is the duty of inspectors of court administration appointed under section 58(1) of the Courts Act 2003 ('the 2003 Act') to inspect and report to the Lord Chancellor on the operation of the coroner system.
(2) Subsection (1) is not to be read as enabling the inspectors –

(a) to inspect persons making judicial decisions or exercising any judicial discretion;
(b) to inspect the Chief Coroner or a Deputy Chief Coroner carrying out any functions as such.

(3) The Chief Inspector appointed under section 58(3) of the 2003 Act must report to the Lord Chancellor on any matter connected with the operation of the coroner system that the Lord Chancellor refers to the Chief Inspector.
(4) An inspector exercising functions under subsection (1) may –

(a) enter any place of work occupied by a senior coroner or the Coroner for Treasure or by an officer or member of staff provided for a senior coroner or the Coroner for Treasure;
(b) inspect and take copies of any records kept by any of those persons that relate to the operation of the coroner system and are considered by the inspector to be relevant to the discharge of his or her functions.

Paragraph 1(3) of Schedule 10 (under which a reference to a senior coroner may include the Chief Coroner) does not apply for the purposes of paragraph (a).

(5) Subsection (4)(a) does not entitle an inspector –

(a) to be present during an inquest, or a part of an inquest, from which people have been excluded by a direction given by virtue of section 45(3);
(b) to attend any private deliberations of persons having jurisdiction to make any determination or finding.

(6) Section 61(4) and (5) of the 2003 Act (records kept on computers) applies to inspections under subsection (4)(b) above as it applies to inspections under section 61(2) of that Act (power to inspect court support system records).
(7) The powers conferred by subsection (4) or by virtue of subsection (6) may be exercised at reasonable times only.
(8) If a report under subsection (1) or (3) recommends the taking of any action by a senior coroner or the Coroner for Treasure, the Lord Chancellor may give a direction requiring the coroner to take the action within a period specified in the direction.

40 Appeals to the Chief Coroner

(1) An interested person may appeal to the Chief Coroner against a decision made by a senior coroner that falls within subsection (2).
(2) The decisions that fall within this subsection are –

- (a) a decision whether to conduct an investigation under this Part into a person's death;
- (b) a decision whether to discontinue an investigation under section 4;
- (c) a decision whether to resume, under Part 2 of Schedule 1, an investigation suspended under Part 1 of that Schedule;
- (d) a decision not to request a post-mortem examination under section 14;
- (e) a decision to request a post-mortem examination under that section of a body that has already been the subject of a post-mortem examination, unless the decision is to request an examination of a different kind from the one already carried out;
- (f) a decision to give a notice under paragraph 1 of Schedule 5;
- (g) a decision whether there should be a jury at an inquest;
- (h) a decision whether to exercise a power conferred by virtue of section 45(3)(a) to exclude persons from all or part of an inquest;
- (i) a decision embodied in a determination as to the questions mentioned in section 5(1)(a) and (b) (read with section 5(2) where applicable);
- (j) a decision embodied in a finding as to the particulars required by the 1953 Act to be registered concerning a death.

(3) An interested person may appeal to the Chief Coroner against a decision made by the Coroner for Treasure (or an Assistant Coroner for Treasure) in connection with –

- (a) an object that is or may be treasure or treasure trove, or
- (b) an investigation or inquest under Chapter 4 concerning such an object,

including a decision embodied in the determination of a question mentioned in section 26(5)(a) or (b).

(4) An interested person may appeal to the Chief Coroner against a failure to make –

- (a) a decision that falls within subsection (2), or
- (b) a decision of a kind mentioned in subsection (3).

(5) A person who the coroner decides is not an interested person may appeal to the Chief Coroner against that decision.
(6) The Lord Chancellor may by order amend subsection (2).
(7) On an appeal under this section the Chief Coroner may consider evidence about any matter that appears to be relevant to the substance of the decision, determination or finding, including evidence that concerns a matter arising after the date of the decision, determination or finding.
(8) On an appeal under this section the Chief Coroner may, if the appeal is allowed, do one or more of the following –

- (a) in the case of an appeal against a decision embodied in a determination or finding –

(i) amend the determination or finding, or
(ii) quash the determination or finding and order a fresh investigation under this Part;

(b) in the case of an appeal against a decision not embodied in a determination or finding –

(i) substitute any other decision that could have been made, or
(ii) quash the decision and remit the matter for a fresh decision;

(c) in the case of an appeal against a failure to make a decision –

(i) make any decision that could have been made, or
(ii) remit the matter for a decision to be made;

(d) make any order (including an order as to costs) that the Chief Coroner thinks appropriate.

(9) A party to an appeal under this section may appeal on a question of law to the Court of Appeal from a decision of the Chief Coroner.
(10) On an appeal under subsection (9) the Court of Appeal may –

(a) affirm the decision;
(b) substitute for the decision any decision that the Chief Coroner could have made;
(c) quash the decision and remit the matter to the Chief Coroner for a fresh decision.

41 Investigation by Chief Coroner or Coroner for Treasure or by judge, former judge or former coroner

Schedule 10 makes provision for an investigation into a person's death to be carried out by the Chief Coroner or the Coroner for Treasure or by a judge, former judge or former coroner.

42 Guidance by the Lord Chancellor

(1) The Lord Chancellor may issue guidance about the way in which the coroner system is expected to operate in relation to interested persons within section 47(2)(a).
(2) Guidance issued under this section may include provision –

(a) about the way in which such persons are able to participate in investigations under this Part into deaths;
(b) about the rights of such persons to appeal under section 40;
(c) about the role of coroners' officers and other staff in helping such persons to participate in investigations and to exercise rights of appeal.

This subsection is not to be read as limiting the power in subsection (1).

(3) The Lord Chancellor may amend or revoke any guidance issued under this section.
(4) The Lord Chancellor must consult the Chief Coroner before issuing, amending or revoking any guidance under this section.

CHAPTER 7 SUPPLEMENTARY

Regulations and rules

43 Coroners regulations

(1) The Lord Chancellor may make regulations –

(a) for regulating the practice and procedure at or in connection with investigations under this Part (other than the practice and procedure at or in connection with inquests);

(b) for regulating the practice and procedure at or in connection with examinations under section 14;
(c) for regulating the practice and procedure at or in connection with exhumations under paragraph 6 of Schedule 5.

Regulations under this section are referred to in this Part as 'Coroners regulations'.

(2) Coroners regulations may be made only if –

(a) the Lord Chief Justice, or
(b) a judicial office holder (as defined in section 109(4) of the Constitutional Reform Act 2005) nominated for the purposes of this subsection by the Lord Chief Justice,

agrees to the making of the regulations.

(3) Coroners regulations may make –

(a) provision for the discharge of an investigation (including provision as to fresh investigations following discharge);
(b) provision for or in connection with the suspension or resumption of investigations;
(c) provision for the delegation by a senior coroner, area coroner or assistant coroner of any of his or her functions;
(d) provision allowing information to be disclosed or requiring information to be given;
(e) provision giving to the Lord Chancellor or the Chief Coroner power to require information from senior coroners;
(f) provision requiring a summary of specified information given to the Chief Coroner by virtue of paragraph (e) to be included in reports under section 36;
(g) provision with respect to the preservation, retention, release or disposal of bodies (including provision with respect to reinterment and with respect to the issue of orders authorising burial);
(h) provision, in relation to authorisations under paragraph 3 of Schedule 5 or entry and search under such authorisations, equivalent to that made by any provision of sections 15 and 16 of the Police and Criminal Evidence Act 1984, subject to any modifications the Lord Chancellor thinks appropriate;
(i) provision, in relation to the power of seizure conferred by paragraph 3(4)(a) of that Schedule, equivalent to that made by any provision of section 21 of that Act, subject to any modifications the Lord Chancellor thinks appropriate;
(j) provision about reports under paragraph 7 of that Schedule.

This subsection is not to be read as limiting the power in subsection (1).

(4) Coroners regulations may apply any provisions of Coroners rules.
(5) Where Coroners regulations apply any provisions of Coroners rules, those provisions –

(a) may be applied to any extent;
(b) may be applied with or without modifications;
(c) may be applied as amended from time to time.

44 Treasure regulations

(1) The Lord Chancellor may make regulations for regulating the practice and procedure at or in connection with investigations under this Part concerning objects that are or may be treasure or treasure trove (other than the practice and procedure at or in connection with inquests concerning such objects).

Regulations under this section are referred to in this Part as 'Treasure regulations'.

(2) Treasure regulations may be made only if –

(a) the Lord Chief Justice, or

(b) a judicial office holder (as defined in section 109(4) of the Constitutional Reform Act 2005) nominated for the purposes of this subsection by the Lord Chief Justice,

agrees to the making of the regulations.

(3) Treasure regulations may make –

(a) provision for the discharge of an investigation (including provision as to fresh investigations following discharge);
(b) provision for or in connection with the suspension or resumption of investigations;
(c) provision for the delegation by the Coroner for Treasure (or an Assistant Coroner for Treasure) of any of his or her functions;
(d) provision allowing information to be disclosed or requiring information to be given;
(e) provision giving to the Lord Chancellor or the Chief Coroner power to require information from the Coroner for Treasure;
(f) provision requiring a summary of specified information given to the Chief Coroner by virtue of paragraph (e) to be included in reports under section 36;
(g) provision of the kind mentioned in paragraph (h) or (i) of section 43(3).

This subsection is not to be read as limiting the power in subsection (1).

(4) Treasure regulations may apply any provisions of Coroners rules.
(5) Where Treasure regulations apply any provisions of Coroners rules, those provisions –

(a) may be applied to any extent;
(b) may be applied with or without modifications;
(c) may be applied as amended from time to time.

45 Coroners rules

(1) Rules may be made in accordance with Part 1 of Schedule 1 to the Constitutional Reform Act 2005 –

(a) for regulating the practice and procedure at or in connection with inquests;
(b) as to the way in which, and the time within which, appeals under section 40(1), (3), (4), (5) or (9) are to be brought;
(c) for regulating the practice and procedure at or in connection with appeals under that section.

Rules under this section are referred to in this Part as 'Coroners rules'.

(2) Coroners rules may make –

(a) provision about evidence (including provision requiring evidence to be given on oath except in prescribed cases);
(b) provision for the discharge of a jury (including provision as to the summoning of new juries following discharge);
(c) provision for the discharge of an inquest (including provision as to fresh inquests following discharge);
(d) provision for or in connection with the adjournment or resumption of inquests;
(e) provision for a senior coroner to have power to give a direction, in proceedings at an inquest, allowing or requiring a name or other matter not to be disclosed except to persons specified in the direction;
(f) provision for the delegation by –

(i) a senior coroner, area coroner or assistant coroner, or
(ii) the Coroner for Treasure (or an Assistant Coroner for Treasure),

of any of his or her functions, except for functions that involve making judicial decisions or exercising any judicial discretion;

(g) provision with respect to the disclosure of information;

(h) provision for persons to be excused from service as jurors at inquests in cases specified in the rules;

(i) provision as to the matters to be taken into account by the Coroner for Treasure in deciding whether to hold an inquest concerning an object that is or may be treasure or treasure trove;

(j) provision for requiring permission to be given for the making of an appeal to the Court of Appeal under any provision of this Part.

(3) Coroners rules may make provision conferring power on a senior coroner or the Coroner for Treasure –

(a) to give a direction excluding specified persons from an inquest, or part of an inquest, if the coroner is of the opinion that the interests of national security so require;

(b) to give a direction excluding specified persons from an inquest during the giving of evidence by a witness under the age of 18, if the coroner is of the opinion that doing so would be likely to improve the quality of the witness's evidence.

In this subsection 'specified persons' means persons of a description specified in the direction, or all persons except those of a description specified in the direction.

(4) Subsections (2) and (3) are not to be read as limiting the power in subsection (1).

(5) Coroners rules may apply –

(a) any provisions of Coroners regulations;

(b) any provisions of Treasure regulations;

(c) any rules of court that relate to proceedings other than inquests.

(6) Where any provisions or rules are applied by virtue of subsection (5), they may be applied –

(a) to any extent;

(b) with or without modifications;

(c) as amended from time to time.

(7) Practice directions may be given in accordance with Part 1 of Schedule 2 to the Constitutional Reform Act 2005 on any matter that could otherwise be included in Coroners rules.

(8) Coroners rules may, instead of providing for a matter, refer to provision made or to be made by practice directions under subsection (7).

(9) In this section 'rules of court' include any provision governing the practice and procedure of a court that is made by or under an enactment.

Coroner of the Queen's household

46 Abolition of the office of coroner of the Queen's household

The office of coroner of the Queen's household is abolished.

Interpretation

47 'Interested person'

(1) This section applies for the purposes of this Part.

(2) 'Interested person', in relation to a deceased person or an investigation or inquest under this Part into a person's death, means –

(a) a spouse, civil partner, partner, parent, child, brother, sister, grandparent, grandchild, child of a brother or sister, stepfather, stepmother, half-brother or half-sister;
(b) a personal representative of the deceased;
(c) a medical examiner exercising functions in relation to the death of the deceased;
(d) a beneficiary under a policy of insurance issued on the life of the deceased;
(e) the insurer who issued such a policy of insurance;
(f) a person who may by any act or omission have caused or contributed to the death of the deceased, or whose employee or agent may have done so;
(g) in a case where the death may have been caused by –

(i) an injury received in the course of an employment, or
(ii) a disease prescribed under section 108 of the Social Security Contributions and Benefits Act 1992 (benefit in respect of prescribed industrial diseases, etc),

a representative of a trade union of which the deceased was a member at the time of death;

(h) a person appointed by, or representative of, an enforcing authority;
(i) where subsection (3) applies, a chief constable;
(j) where subsection (4) applies, a Provost Marshal;
(k) where subsection (5) applies, the Independent Police Complaints Commission;
(l) a person appointed by a Government department to attend an inquest into the death or to assist in, or provide evidence for the purposes of, an investigation into the death under this Part;
(m) any other person who the senior coroner thinks has a sufficient interest.

(3) This subsection applies where it appears that a person has or may have committed –

(a) a homicide offence involving the death of the deceased, or
(b) a related offence (other than a service offence).

(4) This subsection applies where it appears that a person has or may have committed –

(a) the service equivalent of a homicide offence involving the death of the deceased, or
(b) a service offence that is a related offence.

(5) This subsection applies where the death of the deceased is or has been the subject of an investigation managed or carried out by the Independent Police Complaints Commission in accordance with Part 3 of Schedule 3 to the Police Reform Act 2002, including that Part as extended or applied by or under any statutory provision (whenever made).
(6) 'Interested person', in relation to an object that is or may be treasure or treasure trove, or an investigation or inquest under Chapter 4 concerning such an object, means –

(a) the British Museum, if the object was found or is believed to have been found in England;
(b) the National Museum of Wales, if the object was found or is believed to have been found in Wales;
(c) the finder of the object or any person otherwise involved in the find;
(d) the occupier, at the time the object was found, of the land where it was found or is believed to have been found;
(e) a person who had an interest in that land at that time or who has had such an interest since;
(f) any other person who the Coroner for Treasure thinks has a sufficient interest.

(7) For the purposes of this section, a person is the partner of a deceased person if the two of them (whether of different sexes or the same sex) were living as partners in an enduring relationship at the time of the deceased person's death.

48 Interpretation: general

(1) In this Part, unless the context otherwise requires –

'the 1953 Act' means the Births and Deaths Registration Act 1953;

'the 1988 Act' means the Coroners Act 1988;

'active service' means service in –

(a) an action or operation against an enemy (within the meaning given by section 374 of the Armed Forces Act 2006),
(b) an operation outside the British Islands for the protection of life or property, or
(c) the military occupation of a foreign country or territory;

'area', in relation to a senior coroner, area coroner or assistant coroner, means the coroner area for which that coroner is appointed;

'area coroner' means a person appointed under paragraph 2(3) of Schedule 3;

'assistant coroner' means a person appointed under paragraph 2(4) of Schedule 3;

'Assistant Coroner for Treasure' means an assistant coroner, designated under paragraph 7 of Schedule 4, acting in the capacity of Assistant Coroner for Treasure;

'body' includes body parts;

'chief constable' means –

(a) a chief officer of police (within the meaning given in section 101(1) of the Police Act 1996);
(b) the Chief Constable of the Ministry of Defence Police;
(c) the Chief Constable of the Civil Nuclear Constabulary;
(d) the Chief Constable of the British Transport Police;

'the Chief Coroner' means a person appointed under paragraph 1 of Schedule 8;

'the Common Council' means the Common Council of the City of London, and 'common councillor' is to be read accordingly;

'coroner area' is to be read in accordance with paragraph 1 of Schedule 2;

'the Coroner for Treasure' means a person appointed under paragraph 1 of Schedule 4;

'Coroners regulations' means regulations under section 43;

'Coroners rules' means rules under section 45;

'the coroner system' means the system of law and administration relating to investigations and inquests under this Part;

'the court of trial' means –

(a) in relation to an offence (other than a service offence) that is tried summarily, the magistrates' court by which the offence is tried;
(b) in relation to an offence tried on indictment, the Crown Court;
(c) in relation to a service offence, a commanding officer, a Court Martial or the Service Civilian Court (depending on the person before whom, or court before which, it is tried);

'Deputy Chief Coroner' means a person appointed under paragraph 2 of Schedule 8;

'document' includes information stored in an electronic form;

'enforcing authority' has the meaning given by section 18(7) of the Health and Safety at Work etc. Act 1974;

'functions' includes powers and duties;

'homicide offence' has the meaning given in paragraph 1(6) of Schedule 1;

'interested person' is to be read in accordance with section 47;

'land' includes premises within the meaning of the Police and Criminal Evidence Act 1984;

'local authority' means –

(a) in relation to England, a county council, the council of any district comprised in an area for which there is no county council, a London borough council, the Common Council or the Council of the Isles of Scilly;
(b) in relation to Wales, a county council or a county borough council;

'medical examiner' means a person appointed under section 19;

'person', in relation to an offence of corporate manslaughter, includes an organisation;

'prosecuting authority' means –

(a) the Director of Public Prosecutions, or
(b) a person of a description prescribed by an order made by the Lord Chancellor;

'related offence' has the meaning given in paragraph 1(6) of Schedule 1;

'relevant authority', in relation to a coroner area, has the meaning given by paragraph 3 of Schedule 2 (and see paragraph 2 of Schedule 22);

'senior coroner' means a person appointed under paragraph 1 of Schedule 3;

'the service equivalent of a homicide offence' has the meaning given in paragraph 1(6) of Schedule 1;

'service offence' has the meaning given by section 50(2) of the Armed Forces Act 2006 (read without regard to any order under section 380 of that Act) and also includes an offence under –

(a) Part 2 of the Army Act 1955 (3 & 4 Eliz. 2 c. 18) or paragraph 4(6) of Schedule 5A to that Act,
(b) Part 2 of the Air Force Act 1955 (3 & 4 Eliz. 2 c. 19) or paragraph 4(6) of Schedule 5A to that Act, or
(c) Part 1 or section 47K of the Naval Discipline Act 1957 or paragraph 4(6) of Schedule 4A to that Act;

'service police force' means –

(a) the Royal Navy Police,
(b) the Royal Military Police, or
(c) the Royal Air Force Police;

'state detention' has the meaning given by subsection (2);

'statutory provision' means provision contained in, or in an instrument made under, any Act (including this Act);

'treasure' means anything that is treasure for the purposes of the Treasure Act 1996 (and accordingly does not include anything found before 24 September 1997);

'Treasure regulations' means regulations under section 44;

'treasure trove' does not include anything found on or after 24 September 1997.

(2) A person is in state detention if he or she is compulsorily detained by a public authority within the meaning of section 6 of the Human Rights Act 1998.
(3) For the purposes of this Part, the area of the Common Council is to be treated as including the Inner Temple and the Middle Temple.
(4) A reference in this Part to a coroner who is responsible for conducting an investigation under this Part into a person's death is to be read as a reference to the coroner who is under a duty to conduct the investigation, or who would be under such a duty but for the suspension of the investigation under this Part.
(5) A reference in this Part to producing or providing a document, in relation to information stored in an electronic form, is to be read as a reference to producing or providing a copy of the information in a legible form.

Northern Ireland and Scotland amendments

49 Amendments to the Coroners Act (Northern Ireland) 1959

(1) In section 13 of the Coroners Act (Northern Ireland) 1959 (coroner may hold inquest),

in subsection (1), for the words from 'a coroner within whose district' to 'an unexpected or unexplained death' substitute 'a coroner –

(a) who is informed that the body of a deceased person is lying within his district; or

(b) in whose district an unexpected or unexplained death'.

(2) Schedule 11 inserts provisions into the Coroners Act (Northern Ireland) 1959 corresponding to certain provisions in Schedules 5 and 6.

50 Amendments to the Fatal Accidents and Sudden Deaths Inquiry (Scotland) Act 1976

(1) The Fatal Accidents and Sudden Deaths Inquiry (Scotland) Act 1976 is amended as follows.

(2) After section 1 insert –

'1A Death of service personnel abroad

(1) Subsection (4) applies where –

(a) the Lord Advocate is notified under section 12(4) or (5) of the Coroners and Justice Act 2009 in relation to a death,

(b) the death is within subsection (2) or (3), and

(c) the Lord Advocate –

(i) decides that it would be appropriate in the public interest for an inquiry under this Act to be held into the circumstances of the death, and

(ii) does not reverse that decision.

(2) A death is within this subsection if the person who has died was, at the time of the death, in legal custody (as construed by reference to section 1(4)).

(3) A death is within this subsection if it appears to the Lord Advocate that the death –

(a) was sudden, suspicious or unexplained, or

(b) occurred in circumstances such as to give rise to serious public concern.

(4) The procurator fiscal for the appropriate district must –

(a) investigate the circumstances of the death, and

(b) apply to the sheriff for the holding of an inquiry under this Act into those circumstances.

(5) But subsection (4) does not extend to a death within subsection (2) if the Lord Advocate is satisfied that the circumstances of the death have been sufficiently established in the course of any criminal proceedings against any person in respect of the death.

(6) An application under subsection (4)(b) –

(a) is to be made to the sheriff of the appropriate sheriffdom,

(b) must narrate briefly the circumstances of the death so far as known to the procurator fiscal,

(c) may relate to more than one death if the deaths occurred in the same or similar circumstances.

(7) It is for the Lord Advocate to determine the appropriate district and appropriate sheriffdom for the purposes of subsections (4) and (6)(a).'

(3) In section 2 (citation of witnesses for precognition), in subsection (1), after 'section 1(1)' insert 'or 1A(4)'.

(4) In section 3 (holding of public inquiry), in subsections (1) and (3), after 'section 1' insert 'or 1A'.

(5) In section 6 (sheriff's determination etc), in subsection (4)(a)(i), after 'section 1' insert 'or 1A'.

Amendments of Access to Justice Act 1999

51 Public funding for advocacy at certain inquests

(1) Schedule 2 to the Access to Justice Act 1999 (Community Legal Service: excluded cases) is amended as follows.

(2) In paragraph 2, at the end insert ', and

(5) proceedings at an inquest under Part 1 of the Coroners and Justice Act 2009 to which sub-paragraph (1), (2) or (3) of paragraph 4 applies.'

(3) After paragraph 3 there is inserted –

'4 (1) This sub-paragraph applies to an inquest into the death of a person who at the time of the death –

(a) was detained at a custodial institution or in a custody area at a court or police station,
(b) was detained at a removal centre or short-term holding centre,
(c) was being transferred or held in pursuance of prison escort arrangements or immigration escort arrangements,
(d) was detained in secure accommodation,
(e) was a detained patient, or
(f) was in service custody.

(2) This sub-paragraph applies to an inquest into the death of a person that occurred in the course of the person's arrest by a constable or otherwise in the course of the execution or purported execution of any functions by a constable.

(3) This sub-paragraph applies to an inquest into the death of a person who at the time of the death was subject to service law by virtue of section 367 or 369(2)(a) of the Armed Forces Act 2006 and was engaged in active service.

(4) Paragraph 2(5) does not authorise the funding of the provision of services to anyone who is not an interested person within section 47(2)(a) of the Coroners and Justice Act 2009.

(5) In this paragraph –

"active service" means service in –

(a) an action or operation against an enemy (within the meaning given by section 374 of the Armed Forces Act 2006),
(b) an operation outside the British Islands for the protection of life or property, or
(c) the military occupation of a foreign country or territory;

"custodial institution" means a prison, a young offender institution, a secure training centre or a remand centre;

"detained patient" means a person who is detained in any premises under Part 2 or 3 or section 135(3B) or 136(4) of the Mental Health Act 1983;

"immigration escort arrangements" means arrangements made under section 156 of the Immigration and Asylum Act 1999;

"prison escort arrangements" means arrangements made under section 80 of the Criminal Justice Act 1991 or under section 102 or 118 of the Criminal Justice and Public Order Act 1994;

"removal centre" and "short-term holding facility" have the meaning given by section 147 of the Immigration and Asylum Act 1999;

"secure accommodation" means accommodation, not consisting of or forming part of a custodial institution, provided for the purpose of restricting the liberty of persons under the age of 18.'

ooo

PART 9 GENERAL

176 Orders, regulations and rules

(1) Orders or regulations made by the Secretary of State, the Lord Chancellor, the Welsh Ministers or the Chief Coroner under this Act are to be made by statutory instrument.

(2) The Statutory Instruments Act 1946 applies in relation to the power of the Chief Coroner under section 37 to make regulations as if the Chief Coroner were a Minister of the Crown.

(3) Any power conferred by this Act to make orders, regulations or rules includes power –

(a) to make provision generally or only for specified purposes, cases, circumstances or areas;

(b) to make different provision for different purposes, cases, circumstances or areas;

(c) to make incidental, supplementary, consequential, transitional, transitory or saving provision.

(4) A statutory instrument containing an order or regulations under this Act is subject to negative resolution procedure unless it is –

(a) an instrument within subsection (5), or

(b) an instrument containing an order under section 182 only.

(5) A statutory instrument containing (whether alone or with other provision) –

(a) regulations under section 20(5) setting a fee for the first time or increasing the fee by more than is necessary to reflect changes in the value of money,

(b) an order under section 40(6),

(c) an order under section 74, 75, 77 or 78,

(d) an order under section 148(1) or (3),

(e) an order under section 161(2)(a)(ii) or (4),

(f) an order under section 177 which contains provision amending or repealing any provision of an Act, or

(g) an order under paragraph 34 or 35 of Schedule 22,

is subject to affirmative resolution procedure.

(6) In this section –

'affirmative resolution procedure' means –

(a) in relation to any statutory instrument made by the Secretary of State or the Lord Chancellor, a requirement that a draft of the instrument be laid before, and approved by a resolution of, each House of Parliament;

(b) in relation to any statutory instrument made by the Welsh Ministers, a requirement that a draft of the instrument be laid before, and approved by a resolution of, the National Assembly for Wales;

'negative resolution procedure' means –

(a) in relation to any statutory instrument made by the Secretary of State, Lord Chancellor or Chief Coroner, annulment in pursuance of a resolution of either House of Parliament;
(b) in relation to any statutory instrument made by the Welsh Ministers, annulment in pursuance of a resolution of the National Assembly for Wales.

177 Consequential etc amendments and transitional and saving provisions

(1) Schedule 21 contains minor and consequential amendments.
(2) Schedule 22 contains transitional, transitory and saving provisions.
(3) An appropriate minister may by order make –

(a) such supplementary, incidental or consequential provision, or
(b) such transitory, transitional or saving provision,

as the appropriate minister considers appropriate for the general purposes, or any particular purposes, of this Act, or in consequence of, or for giving full effect to, any provision made by this Act.

(4) An order under subsection (3) may, in particular –

(a) provide for any amendment or other provision made by this Act which comes into force before any other provision (whether made by this or any other Act or by any subordinate legislation) has come into force to have effect, until that other provision has come into force, with specified modifications, and
(b) modify any provision of –
    (i) any Act (including this Act and any Act passed in the same session as this Act);
    (ii) subordinate legislation made before the passing of this Act;
    (iii) Northern Ireland legislation passed, or made, before the passing of this Act;
    (iv) any instrument made, before the passing of this Act, under Northern Ireland legislation.

(5) Nothing in this section limits the power, by virtue of section 176(3), to include incidental, supplementary, consequential, transitional, transitory or saving provision in an order under section 182 (commencement).
(6) The modifications that may be made by virtue of subsection (4)(b) are in addition to those made by, or which may be made under, any other provision of this Act.
(7) Her Majesty may by Order in Council extend any provision made by virtue of subsection (4)(b), with such modifications as may appear to Her Majesty to be appropriate, to the Isle of Man or any British overseas territory.
(8) The power under subsection (7) includes power to make supplementary, incidental, consequential, transitory, transitional or saving provision.
(9) Subsection (7) does not apply in relation to amendments of the Armed Forces Act 2006.
(10) In this section –

'appropriate minister' means the Secretary of State or the Lord Chancellor;

'modify' includes amend, repeal and revoke, and modification is to be construed accordingly;

'subordinate legislation' has the same meaning as in the Interpretation Act 1978.

178 Repeals

Schedule 23 contains repeals (including repeals of spent provisions).

179 Financial provision

The following are to be paid out of money provided by Parliament –

(a) any expenditure incurred by a Minister of the Crown under or by virtue of this Act;
(b) any increase attributable to this Act in the sums payable out of money so provided under any other Act.

180 Effect of amendments to provisions applied for purposes of service law

(1) In this section 'relevant criminal justice provisions' means provisions of, or made under, an Act which –

(a) relate to criminal justice, and
(b) are applied (with or without modifications) for any purposes of service law by any provision of, or made under, any Act.

(2) Unless the contrary intention appears, any amendment by this Act of relevant criminal justice provisions also amends those provisions as so applied.
(3) In this section 'service law' means –

(a) the system of service law established by the Armed Forces Act 2006, or
(b) any of the systems of service law superseded by that Act (namely, military law, air force law and the Naval Discipline Act 1957).

181 Extent

(1) Subject to the following provisions of this section and any other provision of this Act, this Act extends to England and Wales only.
(2) The following provisions extend to England and Wales, Scotland and Northern Ireland –

(a) section 84;
(b) the service courts provisions of Chapter 2 of Part 3;
(c) section 143;
(d) Part 7 (except sections 158(1) and (2), 170(2) and 171 and Schedule 19);
(e) sections 176 to 183;
(f) paragraph 4 of Schedule 1;
(g) paragraphs 8, 15, 29, 42 and 45 of Schedule 22.

(3) The following provisions extend to England and Wales and Northern Ireland –

(a) sections 54, 55 and 56(1);
(b) section 61 and Schedule 12;
(c) sections 62 to 66;
(d) section 67(3);
(e) section 68 and Schedule 13;
(f) section 71;
(g) section 73;
(h) Chapter 1 of Part 3 (except section 84);
(i) Chapter 2 of that Part, and paragraphs 16 and 17 of Schedule 22, (subject to subsection (2)(b));
(j) paragraphs 7, 12(2), 39, 40 and 41 of Schedule 22.

(4) The following provisions extend to Northern Ireland only –

(a) section 49 and Schedule 11;
(b) section 67(2);
(c) paragraphs 11, 38 and 44(2) of Schedule 22.

(5) Paragraphs 34 and 35 of Schedule 22 extend to England and Wales and Scotland, and paragraph 36 of that Schedule extends to Scotland only.
(6) Except as otherwise provided by this Act, an amendment, repeal or revocation of any

enactment by any provision of this Act extends to the part or parts of the United Kingdom to which the enactment extends.

(7) In section 338(1) of the Criminal Justice Act 2003 (power to extend the provisions of that Act to the Channel Islands etc) the reference to that Act includes a reference to that Act as amended by any provision of this Act.

(8) In section 384 of the Armed Forces Act 2006 (extent to Channel Islands, Isle of Man etc) any reference to that Act includes a reference to –

(a) that Act as amended by or under any provision of this Act;
(b) section 84;
(c) the service courts provisions of Chapter 2 of Part 3;
(d) section 180.

(9) In section 79(3) of the International Criminal Court Act 2001 (power to extend provisions of that Act to Channel Islands, Isle of Man etc) the reference to that Act includes a reference to that Act as amended by section 70.

(10) In this section 'the service courts provisions of Chapter 2 of Part 3' means the provisions of Chapter 2 of Part 3, and paragraph 70 of Schedule 21 and paragraphs 16 to 22 of Schedule 22, so far as having effect in relation to service courts.

182 Commencement

(1) The following provisions come into force on the day on which this Act is passed –

(a) sections 47 and 48;
(b) section 116;
(c) section 143;
(d) sections 151 and 152;
(e) section 154;
(f) this section and sections 176, 177(3) to (10), 179, 181 and 183;
(g) Schedule 18;
(h) paragraphs 62(3) and 94 to 98 of Schedule 21 (and section 177(1) so far as relating to those provisions);
(i) Part 1 and paragraphs 26 and 47 of Schedule 22 (and section 177(2) so far as relating to those provisions);
(j) in Schedule 23 –

(i) in Part 3, the repeals relating to the Administration of Justice (Miscellaneous Provisions) Act 1933 and the Supreme Court Act 1981,
(ii) in Part 4, the repeals in the Criminal Justice and Immigration Act 2008,
(iii) in Part 5, the repeal of section 8(6) of the Animal Welfare Act 2006,
(iv) in Part 6, the repeals in sections 17 and 17A of, and Schedule 3 to, the Access to Justice Act 1999, and
(v) Part 9,

and section 178 so far as relating to those repeals.

(2) The following provisions come into force at the end of the period of 2 months beginning with the day on which this Act is passed –

(a) section 73;
(b) section 138;
(c) Part 4 of Schedule 21 (and section 177(1) so far as relating to that Part);
(d) paragraph 37 of Schedule 22 (and section 177(2) so far as relating to that provision);
(e) in Part 2 of Schedule 23, the repeals relating to the following Acts –

(i) Libel Act 1792,
(ii) Criminal Libel Act 1819,
(iii) Libel Act 1843,
(iv) Newspaper Libel and Registration Act 1881,

(v) Law of Libel Amendment Act 1888,
(vi) Defamation Act 1952,
(vii) Theatres Act 1968,
(viii) Broadcasting Act 1990,
(ix) Criminal Procedure and Investigations Act 1996,
(x) Defamation Act 1996, and
(xi) Legal Deposit Libraries Act 2003,

and section 178 so far as relating to those repeals.

(3) The following provisions come into force on 1 January 2010 –

(a) Chapter 2 of Part 3;
(b) paragraphs 69 to 71 of Schedule 21 (and section 177(1) so far as relating to those provisions);
(c) paragraphs 16 to 22 of Schedule 22 (and section 177(2) so far as relating to those provisions);
(d) in Part 3 of Schedule 23, the repeals relating to the Criminal Evidence (Witness Anonymity) Act 2008 (and section 178 so far as relating to those repeals).

(4) The following provisions come into force on such day as the Lord Chancellor may by order appoint –

(a) Part 1 (other than sections 19, 20, 21, 47 and 48);
(b) Chapter 1 of Part 4;
(c) sections 146 to 148;
(d) sections 149, 150 and 153;
(e) Parts 1 and 8 of Schedule 21 (and section 177(1) so far as relating to those provisions);
(f) paragraphs 27, 28 and 44 of Schedule 22 (and section 177(2) so far as relating to those provisions);
(g) in Schedule 23 –

(i) the repeals in Part 1,
(ii) the repeals in Part 4 (other than those relating to the Criminal Procedure (Scotland) Act 1995 and the Criminal Justice and Immigration Act 2008), and
(iii) in Part 6, the repeals of section 2(2) of, and paragraph 1(h) of Schedule 2 to, the Access to Justice Act 1999,

and section 178 so far as relating to those repeals.

(5) The other provisions of this Act come into force on such day as the Secretary of State may by order appoint.

183 Short title

This Act may be cited as the Coroners and Justice Act 2009.

SCHEDULES

SCHEDULE 1 DUTY OR POWER TO SUSPEND OR RESUME INVESTIGATIONS

(Section 11)

PART 1 SUSPENSION OF INVESTIGATIONS

Suspension where certain criminal charges may be brought

1 (1) A senior coroner must suspend an investigation under this Part of this Act into a person's death in the following cases.

(2) The first case is where a prosecuting authority requests the coroner to suspend the investigation on the ground that a person may be charged with –

(a) a homicide offence involving the death of the deceased, or
(b) an offence (other than a service offence) that is alleged to be a related offence.

(3) The second case is where a Provost Marshal or the Director of Service Prosecutions requests the coroner to suspend the investigation on the ground that a person may be charged with –

(a) the service equivalent of a homicide offence involving the death of the deceased, or
(b) a service offence that is alleged to be a related offence.

(4) Subject to paragraphs 2 and 3, a suspension of an investigation under this paragraph must be for –

(a) a period of 28 days beginning with the day on which the suspension first takes effect, or
(b) whatever longer period (beginning with that day) the coroner specifies.

(5) The period referred to in sub-paragraph (4) may be extended or further extended –

(a) in the first case, at the request of the authority by which the suspension was originally requested;
(b) in the second case, at the request of –

(i) the Provost Marshal by whom the suspension was originally requested, or
(ii) the Director of Service Prosecutions.

(6) In this Act –

'homicide offence' means –

(a) murder, manslaughter, corporate manslaughter or infanticide;
(b) an offence under any of the following provisions of the Road Traffic Act 1988 –

(i) section 1 (causing death by dangerous driving);
(ii) section 2B (causing death by careless, or inconsiderate, driving);
(iii) section 3ZB (causing death by driving: unlicensed, disqualified or uninsured drivers);
(iv) section 3A (causing death by careless driving when under the influence of drink or drugs);

(c) an offence under section 2(1) of the Suicide Act 1961 (encouraging or assisting suicide);
(d) an offence under section 5 of the Domestic Violence, Crime and Victims Act 2004 (causing or allowing the death of a child or vulnerable adult);

'related offence' means an offence (including a service offence) that –

(a) involves the death of the deceased, but is not a homicide offence or the service equivalent of a homicide offence, or
(b) involves the death of a person other than the deceased (whether or not it is a homicide offence or the service equivalent of a homicide offence) and is committed in circumstances connected with the death of the deceased;

'the service equivalent of a homicide offence' means an offence under section 42 of the Armed Forces Act 2006 (or section 70 of the Army Act 1955 (3 & 4 Eliz. 2 c. 18), section 70 of the Air Force Act 1955 (3 & 4 Eliz. 2 c. 19) or section 42 of the Naval Discipline Act 1957) corresponding to a homicide offence.

Suspension where certain criminal proceedings are brought

2 (1) Subject to sub-paragraph (6), a senior coroner must suspend an investigation under this Part of this Act into a person's death in the following cases.

(2) The first case is where the coroner –

(a) becomes aware that a person has appeared or been brought before a magistrates' court charged with a homicide offence involving the death of the deceased, or

(b) becomes aware that a person has been charged on an indictment with such an offence without having appeared or been brought before a magistrates' court charged with it.

(3) The second case is where the coroner becomes aware that a person has been charged with the service equivalent of a homicide offence involving the death of the deceased.

(4) The third case is where a prosecuting authority informs the coroner that a person –

(a) has appeared or been brought before a magistrates' court charged with an offence (other than a service offence) that is alleged to be a related offence, or

(b) has been charged on an indictment with such an offence without having been sent for trial for it,

and the prosecuting authority requests the coroner to suspend the investigation.

(5) The fourth case is where the Director of Service Prosecutions informs the coroner that a person has been charged with a service offence that is alleged to be a related offence, and the Director requests the coroner to suspend the investigation.

(6) The coroner need not suspend the investigation –

(a) in the first case, if a prosecuting authority informs the coroner that it has no objection to the investigation continuing;

(b) in the second case, if the Director of Service Prosecutions informs the coroner that he or she has no objection to the investigation continuing;

(c) in any case, if the coroner thinks that there is an exceptional reason for not suspending the investigation.

(7) In the case of an investigation that is already suspended under paragraph 1 –

(a) a suspension imposed by virtue of sub-paragraph (2) of that paragraph comes to an end if, in reliance of sub-paragraph (6)(a) above, the coroner decides not to suspend the investigation;

(b) a suspension imposed by virtue of sub-paragraph (3) of that paragraph comes to an end if, in reliance on sub-paragraph (6)(b) above, the coroner decides not to suspend the investigation;

(c) a reference above in this paragraph to suspending an investigation is to be read as a reference to continuing the suspension of an investigation;

(d) if the suspension of the investigation is continued under this paragraph, the investigation is to be treated for the purposes of paragraphs 1(4), 7 and 8 of this Schedule as suspended under this paragraph (and not as suspended under paragraph 1).

Suspension pending inquiry under Inquiries Act 2005

3 (1) Subject to sub-paragraph (2), a senior coroner must suspend an investigation under this Part of this Act into a person's death if –

(a) the Lord Chancellor requests the coroner to do so on the ground that the cause of death is likely to be adequately investigated by an inquiry under the Inquiries Act 2005 that is being or is to be held,

(b) a senior judge has been appointed under that Act as chairman of the inquiry, and

(c) the Lord Chief Justice has indicated approval to the Lord Chancellor, for the purposes of this paragraph, of the appointment of that judge.

In paragraph (b) 'senior judge' means a judge of the High Court or the Court of Appeal or a Justice of the Supreme Court.

(2) The coroner need not suspend the investigation if there appears to be an exceptional reason for not doing so.

(3) In the case of an investigation that is already suspended under paragraph 1 –

(a) a reference above in this paragraph to suspending the investigation is to be read as a reference to continuing the suspension of the investigation;

(b) if the suspension of the investigation is continued under this paragraph, the investigation is to be treated for the purposes of paragraphs 1(4), 7 and 9 of this Schedule as suspended under this paragraph (and not as suspended under paragraph 1).

4 (1) This paragraph applies where an investigation is suspended under paragraph 3 on the basis that the cause of death is likely to be adequately investigated by an inquiry under the Inquiries Act 2005.

(2) The terms of reference of the inquiry must be such that it has as its purpose, or among its purposes, the purpose set out in section 5(1) above (read with section 5(2) where applicable); and section 5 of the Inquiries Act 2005 has effect accordingly.

General power to suspend

5 A senior coroner may suspend an investigation under this Part of this Act into a person's death in any case if it appears to the coroner that it would be appropriate to do so.

Effect of suspension

6 (1) Where an investigation is suspended under this Schedule, the senior coroner must adjourn any inquest that is being held as part of the investigation.

(2) Where an inquest held with a jury is adjourned under this paragraph, the senior coroner may discharge the jury.

PART 2 RESUMPTION OF INVESTIGATIONS

Resumption of investigation suspended under paragraph 1

7 An investigation that is suspended under paragraph 1 must be resumed once the period under sub-paragraph (4) of that paragraph, or as the case may be the extended period under sub-paragraph (5) of that paragraph, has ended.

(But see paragraphs 2(7)(d) and 3(3)(b).)

Resumption of investigation suspended under paragraph 2

8 (1) An investigation that is suspended under paragraph 2 may not be resumed unless, but must be resumed if, the senior coroner thinks that there is sufficient reason for resuming it.

(2) Subject to sub-paragraph (3) –

(a) an investigation that is suspended under paragraph 2 may not be resumed while proceedings are continuing before the court of trial in respect of a homicide offence, or the service equivalent of a homicide offence, involving the death of the deceased;
(b) an investigation that is suspended by virtue of sub-paragraph (4) or (5) of that paragraph may not be resumed while proceedings are continuing before the court of trial in respect of the offence referred to in that sub-paragraph.

(3) The investigation may be resumed while the proceedings in question are continuing if –

(a) in the case of an investigation suspended by virtue of sub-paragraph (2) or (4) of paragraph 2, the relevant prosecuting authority informs the coroner that it has no objection to the investigation being resumed;
(b) in the case of an investigation suspended by virtue of sub-paragraph (3) or (5) of that paragraph, the Director of Service Prosecutions informs the coroner that he or she has no objection to the investigation being resumed.

(4) For the purposes of sub-paragraph (3)(a), the relevant prosecuting authority –

(a) in the case of an investigation suspended by virtue of sub-paragraph (2) of paragraph 2, is the prosecuting authority responsible for the prosecution in question;
(b) in the case of an investigation suspended by virtue of sub-paragraph (4) of that paragraph, is the prosecuting authority that made the request under that sub-paragraph.

(5) In the case of an investigation resumed under this paragraph, a determination under section 10(1)(a) may not be inconsistent with the outcome of –

(a) the proceedings in respect of the charge (or each charge) by reason of which the investigation was suspended;
(b) any proceedings that, by reason of sub-paragraph (2), had to be concluded before the investigation could be resumed.

Resumption of investigation suspended under paragraph 3

9 (1) Where an investigation is suspended under paragraph 3 –

(a) it may not be resumed unless, but must be resumed if, the senior coroner thinks that there is sufficient reason for resuming it;
(b) it may not be resumed before the end of the period of 28 days beginning with the relevant day;
(c) where sub-paragraph (4), (6), (8) or (10) applies, it may be resumed only in accordance with that sub-paragraph (and not before the end of the 28-day period mentioned in paragraph (b)).

(2) In sub-paragraph (1)(b) 'the relevant day' means –

(a) if the Lord Chancellor gives the coroner notification under this paragraph, the day on which the inquiry concerned is concluded;
(b) otherwise, the day on which the findings of that inquiry are published.

(3) Sub-paragraph (4) applies where, during the suspension of the investigation, the coroner –

(a) becomes aware that a person has appeared or been brought before a magistrates' court charged with a homicide offence involving the death of the deceased, or
(b) becomes aware that a person has been charged on an indictment with

such an offence without having appeared or been brought before a magistrates' court charged with it.

(4) The coroner must not resume the investigation until after the conclusion of proceedings before the court of trial in respect of the offence in question, unless a prosecuting authority informs the coroner that it has no objection to the investigation being resumed before then.

(5) Sub-paragraph (6) applies where, during the suspension of the investigation, the coroner becomes aware that a person has been charged with the service equivalent of a homicide offence involving the death of the deceased.

(6) The coroner must not resume the investigation until after the conclusion of proceedings before the court of trial in respect of the offence in question, unless the Director of Service Prosecutions informs the coroner that he or she has no objection to the investigation being resumed before then.

(7) Sub-paragraph (8) applies where, during the suspension of the investigation, a prosecuting authority informs the senior coroner that a person –

(a) has appeared or been brought before a magistrates' court charged with an offence (other than a service offence) that is alleged to be a related offence, or

(b) has been charged on an indictment with such an offence without having been sent for trial for it.

(8) If the prosecuting authority requests the coroner not to resume the investigation until after the conclusion of proceedings before the court of trial in respect of the offence in question, the coroner must not do so.

But the coroner may resume the investigation before the conclusion of those proceedings if the prosecuting authority subsequently informs the coroner that it has no objection to the investigation being resumed before then.

(9) Sub-paragraph (10) applies where the Director of Service Prosecutions informs the coroner that a person has been charged with a service offence that is alleged to be a related offence.

(10) If the Director of Service Prosecutions requests the coroner not to resume the investigation until after the conclusion of proceedings before the court of trial in respect of the offence in question, the coroner must not do so.

But the coroner may resume the investigation before the conclusion of those proceedings if the Director subsequently informs the coroner that he or she has no objection to the investigation being resumed before then.

(11) In the case of an investigation resumed under this paragraph, a determination under section 10(1)(a) may not be inconsistent with the outcome of –

(a) the inquiry under the Inquiries Act 2005 by reason of which the investigation was suspended;

(b) any proceedings that, by reason of sub-paragraph (4), (6), (8) or (10), had to be concluded before the investigation could be resumed.

Resumption of investigation suspended under paragraph 5

10 An investigation that is suspended under paragraph 5 may be resumed at any time if the senior coroner thinks that there is sufficient reason for resuming it.

Supplemental

11 (1) Where an investigation is resumed under this Schedule, the senior coroner must resume any inquest that was adjourned under paragraph 6.

(2) The following provisions apply, in place of section 7, to an inquest that is resumed under this paragraph.

(3) The resumed inquest may be held with a jury if the senior coroner thinks that there is sufficient reason for it to be held with one.

(4) Where the adjourned inquest was held with a jury and the senior coroner decides to hold the resumed inquest with a jury –

(a) if at least seven persons who were members of the original jury are available to serve at the resumed inquest, the resumed inquest must be held with a jury consisting of those persons;

(b) if not, or if the original jury was discharged under paragraph 6(2), a new jury must be summoned.

SCHEDULE 2 CORONER AREAS

(Section 22)

Coroner areas

1 (1) England and Wales is to be divided into areas to be known as coroner areas.

(2) Each coroner area is to consist of the area of a local authority or the combined areas of two or more local authorities.

(3) Subject to paragraph 2 –

(a) the coroner areas are to be those specified in an order made by the Lord Chancellor;

(b) each coroner area is to be known by whatever name is specified in the order.

(4) Before making an order under this paragraph, the Lord Chancellor must consult –

(a) every local authority,

(b) the Welsh Ministers, and

(c) any other persons the Lord Chancellor thinks appropriate.

Alteration of coroner areas

2 (1) The Lord Chancellor may make orders altering coroner areas.

(2) Before making an order under this paragraph the Lord Chancellor must consult –

(a) whichever local authorities the Lord Chancellor thinks appropriate,

(b) in the case of a coroner area in Wales, the Welsh Ministers, and

(c) any other persons the Lord Chancellor thinks appropriate.

(3) 'Altering', in relation to a coroner area, includes (as well as changing its boundaries) –

(a) combining it with one or more other coroner areas;

(b) dividing it between two or more other coroner areas;

(c) changing its name.

Relevant authorities

3 (1) This paragraph sets out for the purposes of this Part what is the 'relevant authority' for a given coroner area.

(2) In the case of a coroner area consisting of the area of a single local authority, that authority is the relevant authority for the coroner area.

(3) In the case of a coroner area consisting of the areas of two or more local authorities, the relevant authority for the coroner area is –

(a) whichever one of those authorities they jointly nominate;
(b) if they cannot agree on a nomination, whichever one of them the Lord Chancellor determines.

(4) Before making a determination under sub-paragraph (3)(b) the Lord Chancellor must consult –

(a) the Secretary of State, in a case involving local authorities in England;
(b) the Welsh Ministers, in a case involving local authorities in Wales.

(5) This paragraph has effect subject to paragraph 2 of Schedule 22.

Effect of body being outside coroner area etc

4 (1) This paragraph applies where –

(a) a senior coroner is responsible for conducting an investigation under this Part into a person's death, and
(b) the body is outside the coroner's area (whether because of its removal or otherwise).

(2) The coroner has the same functions in relation to the body and the investigation as would be the case if the body were within the coroner's area.

(3) The presence of the body at a place outside the coroner's area does not confer any functions on any other coroner.

SCHEDULE 3 APPOINTMENT ETC OF SENIOR CORONERS, AREA CORONERS AND ASSISTANT CORONERS

(Section 23)

PART 1 APPOINTMENT OF SENIOR, AREA AND ASSISTANT CORONERS

Appointment of senior coroners

1 (1) The relevant authority for each coroner area must appoint a coroner (the 'senior coroner') for that area.

(2) In the case of a coroner area that consists of the areas of two or more local authorities, the relevant authority for the area must consult the other authorities before making an appointment under this paragraph.

(3) A person may not be appointed as a senior coroner unless the Lord Chancellor and the Chief Coroner consent to the appointment of that person.

Appointment of area and assistant coroners

2 (1) The Lord Chancellor may by order require the appointment, for any coroner area, of –

(a) an area coroner, or a specified number of area coroners;
(b) a minimum number of assistant coroners.

(2) Before making an order under this paragraph in relation to a particular coroner area, the Lord Chancellor must consult –

(a) the Chief Coroner, and
(b) every local authority whose area falls within the coroner area (or, as the case may be, the local authority whose area is the same as the coroner area).

(3) The relevant authority for a coroner area in relation to which provision is made

under sub-paragraph (1)(a) must appoint an area coroner or, as the case may be, the number of area coroners specified for the area in the order.

(4) The relevant authority for a coroner area in relation to which provision is made under sub-paragraph (1)(b) must appoint at least the number of assistant coroners specified for the area in the order.

(5) A person may not be appointed as an area coroner or assistant coroner unless the Lord Chancellor and the Chief Coroner consent to the appointment of that person.

PART 2 QUALIFICATIONS OF SENIOR, AREA AND ASSISTANT CORONERS

3 To be eligible for appointment as a senior coroner, area coroner or assistant coroner, a person must –

(a) be under the age of 70, and
(b) satisfy the judicial-appointment eligibility condition on a 5-year basis.

4 (1) A person who is a councillor for a local authority, or has been during the previous 6 months, may not be appointed as the senior coroner, or as an area coroner or assistant coroner, for a coroner area that is the same as or includes the area of that local authority.

(2) In the application of this paragraph to the Common Council, the reference to a councillor is to be read as a reference to an alderman of the City of London or a common councillor.

PART 3 VACANCIES; FUNCTIONS OF AREA AND ASSISTANT CORONERS

Filling of vacancies

5 (1) This paragraph applies where a vacancy occurs –

(a) in the office of senior coroner for an area, or
(b) in an office of area coroner for an area.

(2) The relevant authority for the area must –

(a) give notice in writing of the vacancy to the Lord Chancellor and the Chief Coroner as soon as practicable after the vacancy occurs;
(b) appoint a person to fill the vacancy under paragraph 1 or 2 (as the case may be) within 3 months of the vacancy occurring, or within whatever further period the Lord Chancellor allows;
(c) give notice in writing of the appointment of a person to fill the vacancy to the Lord Chancellor and the Chief Coroner as soon as practicable after it is filled.

6 (1) This paragraph applies where –

(a) a vacancy occurs in an office of assistant coroner for an area, and
(b) the vacancy causes the number of assistant coroners for the area to fall below (or further below) the minimum number specified under paragraph 2(1)(b).

(2) Within 3 months of the vacancy occurring, or within whatever further period the Lord Chancellor allows, the relevant authority for the area must appoint a person to fill the vacancy.

Person to act as senior coroner in case of vacancy

7 (1) This paragraph applies where a vacancy occurs in the office of senior coroner for an area.

(2) Subject to sub-paragraph (3), the area coroner for the area (or, if there is more than one such area coroner, whichever of them is nominated by the relevant authority for the area) is to act as senior coroner for the area while the office remains vacant.

(3) Where there is no area coroner for the area, whichever assistant coroner for the area is nominated by the relevant authority for the area is to act as senior coroner for the area while the office remains vacant.

(4) In the case of a coroner area that consists of the area of two or more local authorities, the relevant authority for the area must consult the other authority or authorities before making a nomination under this paragraph.

(5) A person who acts as senior coroner for an area by virtue of this paragraph is to be treated for all purposes of this Part of this Act (except those of this paragraph and paragraphs 1 to 5 and 9 to 19 of this Schedule) as being the senior coroner for the area.

Functions of area and assistant coroners

8 (1) An area coroner or assistant coroner for an area may perform any functions of the senior coroner for the area (including functions which that senior coroner has by virtue of section 2 or 3) –

(a) during a period when that senior coroner is absent or unavailable;
(b) at any other time, with the consent of that senior coroner.

(2) Accordingly a reference in a statutory provision (whenever made) to a senior coroner is to be read, where appropriate, as including an area coroner or assistant coroner.

PART 4 TERMS OF OFFICE OF SENIOR, AREA AND ASSISTANT CORONERS

Status of office

9 The offices of senior coroner, area coroner and assistant coroner are not to be regarded as freehold offices.

Vacation or termination of office

10 A senior coroner, area coroner or assistant coroner must vacate office on reaching the age of 70.

11 (1) The senior coroner or an area coroner or assistant coroner for an area ('the relevant coroner area') must vacate office immediately if –

(a) he or she becomes a councillor for a local authority, and
(b) the area of that local authority is the same as or falls within the relevant coroner area.

(2) In the application of this paragraph to the Common Council, the reference to a councillor is to be read as a reference to an alderman of the City of London or a common councillor.

12 The senior coroner or an area coroner or assistant coroner for an area may resign office by giving notice in writing to the relevant authority for the area. But the resignation does not take effect unless and until it is accepted by the authority.

13 (1) The Lord Chancellor may, with the agreement of the Lord Chief Justice, remove a senior coroner, area coroner or assistant coroner from office for incapacity or misbehaviour.

(2) The Lord Chief Justice may nominate a judicial office holder (as defined in

section 109(4) of the Constitutional Reform Act 2005) to exercise the functions of the Lord Chief Justice under sub-paragraph (1).

Discipline

14 Chapter 3 of Part 4 of the Constitutional Reform Act 2005 (discipline) applies in relation to the offices of senior coroner, area coroner and assistant coroner as it would apply if those offices were listed in Schedule 14 to that Act.

Salary of senior and area coroners

15 (1) The senior coroner for an area is entitled to a salary.

(2) The amount of the salary is to be whatever is from time to time agreed by the senior coroner and the relevant authority for the area.

(3) If the senior coroner and the relevant authority cannot agree about an alteration in the amount of the salary –

(a) either of them may refer the matter to the Lord Chancellor;

(b) the Lord Chancellor may determine the amount of the salary and the date on which it is to become payable.

Any alteration in the amount of salary is to take effect in accordance with the Lord Chancellor's determination.

(4) In making a determination under sub-paragraph (3), the Lord Chancellor must have regard –

(a) to the nature and extent of the coroner's functions, and

(b) to all the circumstances of the case.

(5) The salary to which the senior coroner for an area is entitled under this paragraph is payable by the relevant authority for the area.

(6) This paragraph applies in relation to an area coroner for an area as it applies in relation to the senior coroner for an area (references to the senior coroner being read as references to an area coroner).

Fees payable to assistants

16 (1) An assistant coroner for an area is entitled to fees.

(2) The amount of the fees is to be whatever is agreed from time to time by the assistant coroner and the relevant authority for the area.

(3) The fees to which an assistant coroner for an area is entitled under this paragraph are payable by the relevant authority for the area.

Pensions for senior and area coroners

17 A relevant authority for a coroner area must make provision for the payment of pensions, allowances or gratuities to or in respect of persons who are or have been senior coroners or area coroners for the area.

Prohibition on receipt of fees etc

18 Except as permitted by or under this or any other Act, a senior coroner, area coroner or assistant coroner may not accept any remuneration or fee in respect of anything done by that coroner in the performance of his or her functions.

Other terms of office

19 Subject to the preceding provisions of this Part, the senior coroner or an area coroner or assistant coroner for an area holds office on whatever terms are from time to time agreed by that coroner and the relevant authority for the area.

SCHEDULE 4 CORONER FOR TREASURE AND ASSISTANT CORONERS FOR TREASURE

(Section 25)

PART 1 APPOINTMENT, QUALIFICATIONS AND TERMS OF OFFICE OF CORONER FOR TREASURE

Appointment

1 The Lord Chancellor may appoint a person as the Coroner for Treasure.

Qualifications

2 To be eligible for appointment as the Coroner for Treasure, a person must –

(a) be under the age of 70, and
(b) satisfy the judicial-appointment eligibility condition on a 5-year basis.

Vacation or termination of office

3 The Coroner for Treasure must vacate office on reaching the age of 70.
4 The Coroner for Treasure may resign office by giving notice to the Lord Chancellor. But the resignation does not take effect unless and until it is accepted by the Lord Chancellor.

5 (1) The Lord Chancellor may, with the agreement of the Lord Chief Justice, remove the Coroner for Treasure from office for incapacity or misbehaviour.
(2) The Lord Chief Justice may nominate a judicial office holder (as defined in section 109(4) of the Constitutional Reform Act 2005) to exercise the functions of the Lord Chief Justice under sub-paragraph (1).

Remuneration, allowances and expenses

6 (1) The Lord Chancellor may pay to the Coroner for Treasure amounts determined by the Lord Chancellor by way of remuneration or allowances.
(2) The Lord Chancellor may pay to the Coroner for Treasure amounts determined by the Lord Chancellor towards expenses incurred by the Coroner for Treasure in performing functions as such.

PART 2 DESIGNATION AND REMUNERATION OF ASSISTANT CORONERS FOR TREASURE

Designation

7 The Chief Coroner may designate one or more assistant coroners to act as Assistant Coroners for Treasure.
8 A person who is designated under paragraph 7 to act as an Assistant Coroner for Treasure may act as such for so long as the designation continues to have effect.
9 A person's designation under that paragraph ceases to have effect –

(a) when the person ceases to be an assistant coroner;
(b) if earlier, when the designation is terminated by notice given –

(i) by the person to the Chief Coroner, or
(ii) by the Chief Coroner to the person.

Remuneration, allowances and expenses

10 (1) The Lord Chancellor may pay to an Assistant Coroner for Treasure amounts determined by the Lord Chancellor by way of remuneration or allowances.

(2) The Lord Chancellor may pay to an Assistant Coroner for Treasure amounts determined by the Lord Chancellor towards expenses incurred by the Assistant Coroner for Treasure in performing functions as such.

PART 3 MISCELLANEOUS

Functions of Assistant Coroners for Treasure

11 (1) An Assistant Coroner for Treasure may perform any functions of the Coroner for Treasure –

(a) during a period when the Coroner for Treasure is absent or unavailable;
(b) during a vacancy in the office of Coroner for Treasure;
(c) at any other time, with the consent of the Coroner for Treasure.

(2) Accordingly a reference in this Part of this Act to the Coroner for Treasure is to be read, where appropriate, as including an Assistant Coroner for Treasure.

Staff

12 (1) The Lord Chancellor may appoint staff to assist the Coroner for Treasure and any Assistant Coroners for Treasure in the performance of their functions.

(2) Such staff are to be appointed on whatever terms and conditions the Lord Chancellor thinks appropriate.

SCHEDULE 5 POWERS OF CORONERS

(Section 32)

Power to require evidence to be given or produced

1 (1) A senior coroner may by notice require a person to attend at a time and place stated in the notice and –

(a) to give evidence at an inquest,
(b) to produce any documents in the custody or under the control of the person which relate to a matter that is relevant to an inquest, or
(c) to produce for inspection, examination or testing any other thing in the custody or under the control of the person which relates to a matter that is relevant to an inquest.

(2) A senior coroner who is conducting an investigation under this Part may by notice require a person, within such period as the senior coroner thinks reasonable –

(a) to provide evidence to the senior coroner, about any matters specified in the notice, in the form of a written statement,
(b) to produce any documents in the custody or under the control of the person which relate to a matter that is relevant to the investigation, or
(c) to produce for inspection, examination or testing any other thing in the custody or under the control of the person which relates to a matter that is relevant to the investigation.

(3) A notice under sub-paragraph (1) or (2) must –

(a) explain the possible consequences, under paragraphs 6 and 7 of Schedule 6, of not complying with the notice;

(b) indicate what the recipient of the notice should do if he or she wishes to make a claim under sub-paragraph (4).

(4) A claim by a person that –

(a) he or she is unable to comply with a notice under this paragraph, or
(b) it is not reasonable in all the circumstances to require him or her to comply with such a notice,

is to be determined by the senior coroner, who may revoke or vary the notice on that ground.

(5) In deciding whether to revoke or vary a notice on the ground mentioned in sub-paragraph (4)(b), the senior coroner must consider the public interest in the information in question being obtained for the purposes of the inquest or investigation, having regard to the likely importance of the information.

(6) For the purposes of this paragraph a document or thing is under a person's control if it is in the person's possession or if he or she has a right to possession of it.

(7) The validity of a notice under sub-paragraph (1) or (2) is not limited to the coroner area for which the senior coroner issuing the notice is appointed.

(8) A reference in this paragraph to a senior coroner is to be read as including the Coroner for Treasure.
As it applies in relation to the Coroner for Treasure, this paragraph has effect with the omission of sub-paragraph (7).

2 (1) A person may not be required to give, produce or provide any evidence or document under paragraph 1 if –

(a) he or she could not be required to do so in civil proceedings in a court in England and Wales, or
(b) the requirement would be incompatible with a Community obligation.

(2) The rules of law under which evidence or documents are permitted or required to be withheld on grounds of public interest immunity apply in relation to an investigation or inquest under this Part as they apply in relation to civil proceedings in a court in England and Wales.

Power of entry, search and seizure

3 (1) A senior coroner conducting an investigation under this Part, if authorised –

(a) by the Chief Coroner, or
(b) by another senior coroner nominated by the Chief Coroner to give authorisation,

may enter and search any land specified in the authorisation.

(2) An authorisation may be given only if –

(a) the senior coroner conducting the investigation has reason to suspect that there may be anything on the land which relates to a matter that is relevant to the investigation, and
(b) any of the conditions in sub-paragraph (3) are met.

(3) Those conditions are –

(a) that it is not practicable to communicate with a person entitled to grant permission to enter and search the land;
(b) that permission to enter and search the land has been refused;
(c) that the senior coroner has reason to believe that such permission would be refused if requested;

(d) that the purpose of a search may be frustrated or seriously prejudiced unless the senior coroner can secure immediate entry to the land on arrival.

(4) A senior coroner conducting an investigation under this Part who is lawfully on any land –

(a) may seize anything that is on the land;
(b) may inspect and take copies of any documents.

(5) A reference in this paragraph to land is not limited to land within the coroner area for which the senior coroner in question is appointed.

(6) A reference in this paragraph to a senior coroner is to be read as including the Coroner for Treasure. As it applies in relation to the Coroner for Treasure, this paragraph has effect with the omission of sub-paragraphs (1)(b) and (5).

4 (1) The person by whom an authorisation under paragraph 3(1) is given must make a record –

(a) setting out the reasons for the suspicion referred to in paragraph 3(2)(a);
(b) specifying which of the conditions in paragraph 3(3) is met.

(2) Where the authorisation is given by a senior coroner nominated under paragraph 3(1)(b), that coroner must give the record made under this paragraph to the Chief Coroner.

(3) The Chief Coroner must retain a record made [under] this paragraph until the Chief Coroner has given to the Lord Chancellor the report under section 36 for the calendar year in which the authorisation in question was given.

5 (1) A power under paragraph 3(4) is not exercisable unless the person exercising the power has reasonable grounds for believing –

(a) that its exercise may assist the investigation, and
(b) in the case of the seizure of anything, that the seizure is necessary to prevent the thing being concealed, lost, damaged, altered or destroyed.

(2) The power under paragraph 3(4)(b) includes power to require any information that is stored in an electronic form and is on, or accessible from, the land to be produced in a form –

(a) in which it can be taken away, and
(b) in which it is legible or from which it can readily be produced in a legible form.

(3) A power under paragraph 3(4) does not apply to any item that the person by whom the power is exercisable has reasonable grounds for believing to be subject to legal privilege.

(4) Anything that has been seized or taken away under paragraph 3 may be retained for so long as is necessary in all the circumstances.

(5) A person on whom a power is conferred by virtue of paragraph 3 may use reasonable force, if necessary, in the exercise of the power.

(6) In this paragraph 'subject to legal privilege', in relation to an item, has the meaning given by section 10 of the Police and Criminal Evidence Act 1984.

Exhumation of body for examination

6 (1) A senior coroner may order the exhumation of a person's body if sub-paragraph (2) or (3) applies.

(2) This sub-paragraph applies if –

(a) the body is buried in England and Wales (whether or not within the coroner area for which the coroner is appointed), and

(b) the coroner thinks it necessary for the body to be examined under section 14.

(3) This sub-paragraph applies if –

(a) the body is buried within the coroner area for which the coroner is appointed, and
(b) the coroner thinks it necessary for the body to be examined for the purpose of any criminal proceedings that have been instituted or are contemplated in respect of –

(i) the death of the person whose body it is, or
(ii) the death of another person who died in circumstances connected with the death of that person.

(4) In sub-paragraph (3) 'criminal proceedings' includes proceedings in respect of an offence under section 42 of the Armed Forces Act 2006 (or section 70 of the Army Act 1955, section 70 of the Air Force Act 1955 or section 42 of the Naval Discipline Act 1957).

Action to prevent other deaths

7 (1) Where –

(a) a senior coroner has been conducting an investigation under this Part into a person's death,
(b) anything revealed by the investigation gives rise to a concern that circumstances creating a risk of other deaths will occur, or will continue to exist, in the future, and
(c) in the coroner's opinion, action should be taken to prevent the occurrence or continuation of such circumstances, or to eliminate or reduce the risk of death created by such circumstances,

the coroner must report the matter to a person who the coroner believes may have power to take such action.

(2) A person to whom a senior coroner makes a report under this paragraph must give the senior coroner a written response to it.
(3) A copy of a report under this paragraph, and of the response to it, must be sent to the Chief Coroner.

SCHEDULE 6 OFFENCES

(Section 33)

PART 1 OFFENCES RELATING TO JURORS

1 (1) It is an offence for a person to serve on a jury at an inquest if the person –

(a) is disqualified from jury service (by reason of being a person listed in Part 2 of Schedule 1 to the Juries Act 1974), and
(b) knows that he or she is disqualified from jury service.

(2) A person guilty of an offence under this paragraph is liable on summary conviction to a fine not exceeding level 5 on the standard scale.

2 (1) It is an offence for a person –

(a) to refuse without reasonable excuse to answer any question put under section 8(5),
(b) to give an answer to such a question knowing the answer to be false in a material particular, or

(c) recklessly to give an answer to such a question that is false in a material particular.

(2) A person guilty of an offence under this paragraph is liable on summary conviction to a fine not exceeding level 3 on the standard scale.

3 (1) It is an offence for a person who is duly summoned as a juror at an inquest –

(a) to make any false representation, or
(b) to cause or permit to be made any false representation on his or her behalf,

with the intention of evading service as a juror at an inquest.

(2) A person guilty of an offence under this paragraph is liable on summary conviction to a fine not exceeding level 3 on the standard scale.

4 (1) It is an offence for a person to make or cause to be made, on behalf of a person who has been duly summoned as a juror at an inquest, any false representation with the intention of enabling the other person to evade service as a juror at an inquest.

(2) A person guilty of an offence under this paragraph is liable on summary conviction to a fine not exceeding level 3 on the standard scale.

5 (1) A senior coroner, or (as the case may be) the Coroner for Treasure, may impose a fine not exceeding £1000 on a person duly summoned as a juror at an inquest who –

(a) fails without reasonable excuse to attend in accordance with the summons, or
(b) attends in accordance with the summons but refuses without reasonable excuse to serve as a juror.

(2) But a fine may not be imposed under this paragraph unless the summons was duly served on the person in question not later than 14 days before the day on which he or she was required to attend.

PART 2 OFFENCES RELATING TO WITNESSES AND EVIDENCE

6 A senior coroner, or (as the case may be) the Coroner for Treasure, may impose a fine not exceeding £1000 on a person who fails without reasonable excuse to do anything required by a notice under paragraph 1 of Schedule 5.

7 (1) It is an offence for a person to do anything that is intended to have the effect of –

(a) distorting or otherwise altering any evidence, document or other thing that is given, produced or provided for the purposes of an investigation under this Part of this Act, or
(b) preventing any evidence, document or other thing from being given, produced or provided for the purposes of such an investigation,

or to do anything that the person knows or believes is likely to have that effect.

(2) It is an offence for a person –

(a) intentionally to suppress or conceal a document that is, and that the person knows or believes to be, a relevant document, or
(b) intentionally to alter or destroy such a document.

(3) For the purposes of sub-paragraph (2) a document is a 'relevant document' if it is likely that a person conducting an investigation under this Part of this Act would (if aware of its existence) wish to be provided with it.

(4) A person does not commit an offence under sub-paragraph (1) or (2) by doing anything that is authorised or required –

(a) by a senior coroner or the Coroner for Treasure, or
(b) by virtue of paragraph 2 of Schedule 5 or any privilege that applies.

(5) Proceedings for an offence under sub-paragraph (1) or (2) may be instituted only by or with the consent of the Director of Public Prosecutions.

(6) A person guilty of an offence under sub-paragraph (1) or (2) is liable on summary conviction to a fine not exceeding level 3 on the standard scale, or to imprisonment for a term not exceeding 51 weeks, or to both.

8 (1) It is an offence for a person, in giving unsworn evidence at an inquest by virtue of section 45(2)(a), to give false evidence in such circumstances that, had the evidence been given on oath, he or she would have been guilty of perjury.

(2) A person guilty of an offence under this paragraph is liable on summary conviction to a fine not exceeding £1000, or to imprisonment for a term not exceeding 51 weeks, or to both.

(3) In relation to a person under the age of 14, sub-paragraph (2) has effect as if for the words following 'summary conviction' there were substituted 'to a fine not exceeding £250'.

(4) For the purposes of sub-paragraph (3), a person's age is to be taken to be that which it appears to the court to be after considering any available evidence.

PART 3 MISCELLANEOUS

9 (1) The powers of a senior coroner or the Coroner for Treasure under paragraph 5 or 6 are additional to, and do not affect, any other power the coroner may have –

(a) to compel a person to appear before him or her;
(b) to compel a person to give evidence or produce any document or other thing;
(c) to punish a person for contempt of court for failure to appear or to give evidence or to produce any document or other thing.

(2) But a person may not be fined under paragraph 5 or 6 and also be punished under any such other power.

10 In relation to an offence committed before the commencement of section 281(5) of the Criminal Justice Act 2003, a reference in this Schedule to 51 weeks is to be read as a reference to 6 months.

SCHEDULE 7 ALLOWANCES, FEES AND EXPENSES

(Section 34)

PART 1 ALLOWANCES PAYABLE TO JURORS

1 A person who serves as a juror at an inquest is entitled, in respect of attending the inquest, to receive payments by way of allowance –

(a) for travelling and subsistence;
(b) for financial loss.

This is subject to any conditions prescribed by regulations.

2 But a person is entitled to receive payments by way of allowance for financial loss only if, in consequence of attending the inquest, the person has –

(a) incurred expenses (other than on travelling and subsistence) that he or she would otherwise not have incurred,
(b) suffered a loss of earnings that he or she would otherwise not have suffered, or
(c) suffered a loss of benefit under the enactments relating to social security that he or she would otherwise not have suffered.

3 Regulations may prescribe the rates of any allowances payable under paragraph 1.

4 The amount due to a person under paragraph 1 is to be calculated by the senior coroner and paid by (or on behalf of) the senior coroner or, where appropriate, the Coroner for Treasure.

PART 2 ALLOWANCES PAYABLE TO WITNESSES

5 (1) Regulations may prescribe the allowances that may be paid by (or on behalf of) senior coroners or the Coroner for Treasure –

(a) to witnesses;

(b) to persons who produce documents or things by virtue of paragraph 1(1) or (2) of Schedule 5;

(c) to persons who provide evidence in the form of a written statement by virtue of paragraph 1(2)(a) of that Schedule.

(2) In this paragraph 'witness' means a person properly attending before a senior coroner to give evidence at an inquest or in connection with the possibility of doing so (whether or not the person actually gives evidence), but does not include –

(a) a police officer, or a member of a service police force, attending in his or her capacity as such;

(b) a full-time officer of an institution to which the Prison Act 1952 applies in his or her capacity as such;

(c) a prisoner in respect of an occasion on which he or she is conveyed in custody to appear before a senior coroner.

PART 3 MISCELLANEOUS FEES, ALLOWANCES AND EXPENSES

6 Regulations may prescribe the fees and allowances that may be paid by (or on behalf of) senior coroners to persons who make examinations under section 14.

7 (1) A relevant authority for a coroner area may issue a schedule of the fees, allowances and expenses that may be lawfully paid or incurred by the senior coroner for the area in the performance of the coroner's functions.

(2) The power under sub-paragraph (1) includes power to amend or revoke any schedule issued.

(3) In exercising the power under sub-paragraph (1) a relevant authority must have regard to any guidance from time to time issued by the Lord Chancellor.

(4) A copy of any schedule that is issued or amended must be given to the senior coroner.

(5) The reference in sub-paragraph (1) to fees and allowances does not include fees or allowances within any of the preceding paragraphs of this Schedule.

8 Regulations may prescribe the fees payable to coroners for supplying copies of documents in their custody relating to investigations or inquests under this Part of this Act that they are conducting or have conducted.

PART 4 MEETING OR REIMBURSING EXPENSES

9 (1) Regulations may make provision for or in connection with meeting or reimbursing –

(a) expenses incurred by senior coroners (including expenses incurred under or by virtue of paragraph 4, 5 or 6);

(b) expenses incurred by area coroners and assistant coroners;

(c) expenses incurred by virtue of Schedule 10 in the conduct of an investigation by the Chief Coroner or the Coroner for Treasure or by a judge, former judge or former coroner.

(2) The regulations may make provision –

(a) for accounts or evidence relating to expenses to be provided to relevant authorities;
(b) for or in connection with the meeting or reimbursement by relevant authorities of expenses of a description specified in the regulations;
(c) for or in connection with appeals relating to decisions with respect to meeting or reimbursing expenses.

This sub-paragraph is not to be read as limiting the power in sub-paragraph (1).

(3) A reference in this paragraph to meeting or reimbursing expenses incurred by a person ('P') includes a reference to indemnifying P in respect of –

(a) costs that P reasonably incurs in or in connection with proceedings in respect of things done or omitted in the exercise (or purported exercise) by P of duties under this Part of this Act;
(b) costs that P reasonably incurs in taking steps to dispute claims that might be made in such proceedings;
(c) damages awarded against P, or costs ordered to be paid by P, in such proceedings;
(d) sums payable by P in connection with a reasonable settlement of such proceedings or of claims that might be made in such proceedings.

PART 5 SUPPLEMENTAL

10 For the purposes of paragraph 1, a person who attends for service as a juror in accordance with a summons is to be treated as serving as a juror even if he or she is not sworn.

11 (1) The power to make regulations under this Schedule is exercisable by the Lord Chancellor.

(2) Regulations under this Schedule may be made only if –

(a) the Lord Chief Justice, or
(b) a judicial office holder (as defined in section 109(4) of the Constitutional Reform Act 2005) nominated for the purposes of this sub-paragraph by the Lord Chief Justice,

agrees to the making of the regulations.

SCHEDULE 8 CHIEF CORONER AND DEPUTY CHIEF CORONERS

(Section 35)

Appointment of Chief Coroner

1 (1) The Lord Chief Justice may appoint a person as the Chief Coroner.

(2) To be eligible for appointment as the Chief Coroner a person must be –

(a) a judge of the High Court or a Circuit judge, and
(b) under the age of 70.

(3) The Lord Chief Justice must consult the Lord Chancellor before making an appointment under this paragraph.

(4) The appointment of a person as the Chief Coroner is to be for a term decided by

the Lord Chief Justice after consulting the Lord Chancellor. The term must be one that expires before the person's 70th birthday.

(5) In this paragraph 'appointment' includes re-appointment.

Appointment of Deputy Chief Coroners

2 (1) The Lord Chief Justice may secure the appointment as Deputy Chief Coroners of however many persons the Lord Chief Justice thinks appropriate.

(2) To be eligible for appointment as a Deputy Chief Coroner a person must be –

(a) a judge of the High Court, a Circuit judge, the Coroner for Treasure or a senior coroner, and

(b) under the age of 70.

(3) The Lord Chief Justice must consult the Lord Chancellor as to –

(a) the appropriate number of persons to be appointed as Deputy Chief Coroners;

(b) how many of them are to be persons eligible for appointment by virtue of being judges and how many are to be persons eligible for appointment by virtue of being senior coroners or the Coroner for Treasure.

(4) The function of appointing a person as a Deputy Chief Coroner is exercisable, in the case of a judge of the High Court or a Circuit judge, by the Lord Chief Justice after consulting the Lord Chancellor.

(5) The appointment by the Lord Chief Justice of a person as a Deputy Chief Coroner is to be for a term decided by the Lord Chief Justice after consulting the Lord Chancellor.

The term must be one that expires before the person's 70th birthday.

(6) The function of appointing a person as a Deputy Chief Coroner is exercisable, in the case of a senior coroner or the Coroner for Treasure, by the Lord Chancellor at the invitation of the Lord Chief Justice.

(7) The appointment by the Lord Chancellor of a person as a Deputy Chief Coroner is to be for a term decided by the Lord Chancellor after consulting the Lord Chief Justice.

The term must be one that expires before the person's 70th birthday.

(8) In this paragraph 'appointment' includes re-appointment.

Resignation or removal

3 (1) The Chief Coroner, or a Deputy Chief Coroner appointed by the Lord Chief Justice, may resign from office by giving notice in writing to the Lord Chief Justice.

(2) But the resignation does not take effect unless and until it is accepted by the Lord Chief Justice, who must consult the Lord Chancellor before accepting it.

(3) A Deputy Chief Coroner appointed by the Lord Chancellor may resign from office by giving notice in writing to the Lord Chancellor.

(4) But the resignation does not take effect unless and until it is accepted by the Lord Chancellor, who must consult the Lord Chief Justice before accepting it.

4 (1) The Lord Chief Justice may, after consulting the Lord Chancellor, remove the Chief Coroner, or a Deputy Chief Coroner appointed by the Lord Chief Justice, from office for incapacity or misbehaviour.

(2) The Lord Chancellor may, after consulting the Lord Chief Justice, remove a Deputy Chief Coroner appointed by the Lord Chancellor from office for incapacity or misbehaviour.

Remuneration, allowances and expenses

5 The Lord Chancellor may pay to the Chief Coroner –

(a) amounts determined by the Lord Chancellor by way of remuneration or allowances;

(b) amounts determined by the Lord Chancellor towards expenses incurred by the Chief Coroner in performing functions as such.

6 The Lord Chancellor may pay to a Deputy Chief Coroner –

(a) amounts determined by the Lord Chancellor by way of remuneration or allowances;

(b) amounts determined by the Lord Chancellor towards expenses incurred by that Deputy Chief Coroner in performing functions as such.

7 A reference in paragraph 5 or 6 to paying expenses incurred by a person ('P') includes a reference to indemnifying P in respect of –

(a) costs that P reasonably incurs in or in connection with proceedings in respect of things done or omitted in the exercise (or purported exercise) by P of duties under this Part;

(b) costs that P reasonably incurs in taking steps to dispute claims that might be made in such proceedings;

(c) damages awarded against P, or costs ordered to be paid by P, in such proceedings;

(d) sums payable by P in connection with a reasonable settlement of such proceedings or of claims that might be made in such proceedings.

Exercise of Chief Coroner's functions by Deputy Chief Coroner

8 (1) A Deputy Chief Coroner may perform any functions of the Chief Coroner –

(a) during a period when the Chief Coroner is absent or unavailable;

(b) during a vacancy in the office of Chief Coroner;

(c) at any other time, with the consent of the Chief Coroner.

(2) Accordingly a reference in this Part to the Chief Coroner is to be read, where appropriate, as including a Deputy Chief Coroner.

Staff

9 (1) The Lord Chancellor must appoint staff to assist the Chief Coroner and any Deputy Chief Coroners in the performance of their functions.

(2) Such staff are to be appointed on whatever terms and conditions the Lord Chancellor thinks appropriate.

SCHEDULE 9 MEDICAL ADVISER AND DEPUTY MEDICAL ADVISERS TO THE CHIEF CORONER

(Section 38)

Appointment and functions of Medical Adviser to the Chief Coroner

1 The Lord Chancellor may appoint a person as Medical Adviser to the Chief Coroner ('the Medical Adviser') to provide advice and assistance to the Chief Coroner as to medical matters in relation to the coroner system.

Appointment and functions of Deputy Medical Advisers to the Chief Coroner

2 (1) The Lord Chancellor may appoint however many Deputy Medical Advisers to the Chief Coroner ('Deputy Medical Advisers') the Lord Chancellor thinks appropriate.

(2) A Deputy Medical Adviser may perform any functions of the Medical Adviser –

(a) during a period when the Medical Adviser is absent or unavailable;
(b) during a vacancy in the office of Medical Adviser;
(c) at any other time, with the consent of the Medical Adviser.

Qualification for appointment

3 A person may be appointed as the Medical Adviser or as a Deputy Medical Adviser only if, at the time of the appointment, he or she –

(a) is a registered medical practitioner and has been throughout the previous 5 years, and
(b) practises as such or has done within the previous 5 years.

Consultation before making appointment

4 Before appointing a person as the Medical Adviser or as a Deputy Medical Adviser, the Lord Chancellor must consult –

(a) the Chief Coroner, and
(b) the Welsh Ministers.

Terms and conditions of appointment

5 The appointment of a person as the Medical Adviser or as a Deputy Medical Adviser is to be on whatever terms and conditions the Lord Chancellor thinks appropriate.

Remuneration, allowances and expenses

6 (1) The Lord Chancellor may pay to the Medical Adviser –

(a) amounts determined by the Lord Chancellor by way of remuneration or allowances;
(b) amounts determined by the Lord Chancellor towards expenses incurred in performing functions as such.

(2) The Lord Chancellor may pay to a Deputy Medical Adviser –

(a) amounts determined by the Lord Chancellor by way of remuneration or allowances;
(b) amounts determined by the Lord Chancellor towards expenses incurred by that Deputy Medical Adviser in performing functions as such.

SCHEDULE 10 INVESTIGATION BY CHIEF CORONER OR CORONER FOR TREASURE OR BY JUDGE, FORMER JUDGE OR FORMER CORONER

(Section 41)

Investigation by Chief Coroner

1 (1) The Chief Coroner may conduct an investigation into a person's death.
(2) Where the Chief Coroner is responsible for conducting an investigation by virtue of this paragraph –

(a) the Chief Coroner has the same functions in relation to the body and the investigation as would be the case if he or she were a senior coroner in whose area the body was situated;
(b) no senior coroner, area coroner or assistant coroner has any functions in relation to the body or the investigation.

(3) Accordingly a reference in a statutory provision (whenever made) to a senior coroner is to be read, where appropriate, as including the Chief Coroner exercising functions by virtue of this paragraph.

Investigation by Coroner for Treasure

2 (1) The Chief Coroner may direct the Coroner for Treasure to conduct an investigation into a person's death.

(2) Where a direction is given under this paragraph –

(a) the Coroner for Treasure must conduct the investigation;
(b) the Coroner for Treasure has the same functions in relation to the body and the investigation as would be the case if he or she were a senior coroner in whose area the body was situated;
(c) no senior coroner, area coroner or assistant coroner has any functions in relation to the body or the investigation.

(3) Accordingly, a reference in a statutory provision (whenever made) to a senior coroner is to be read, where appropriate, as including the Coroner for Treasure exercising functions by virtue of this paragraph.

Investigation by judge, former judge or former coroner

3 (1) If requested to do so by the Chief Coroner, the Lord Chief Justice may nominate a person within sub-paragraph (2) to conduct an investigation into a person's death.

(2) A person is within this sub-paragraph if at the time of the nomination he or she is –

(a) a judge of the High Court,
(b) a Circuit judge, or
(c) a person who has held office as a judge of the Court of Appeal or of the High Court (but no longer does so),

and is under the age of 75.

(3) The Chief Coroner may request a person who at the time of the request –

(a) has held office as a senior coroner (but no longer does so), and
(b) is under the age of 75,

to conduct an investigation into a person's death.

(4) If a person nominated or requested under this paragraph agrees to conduct the investigation –

(a) that person is under a duty to do so;
(b) that person has the same functions in relation to the body and the investigation as would be the case if he or she were a senior coroner in whose area the body was situated;
(c) no senior coroner, area coroner or assistant coroner has any functions in relation to the body or the investigation.

(5) Accordingly a reference in a statutory provision (whenever made) to a coroner is to be read, where appropriate, as including a person who has been nominated or requested under this paragraph to conduct an investigation and has agreed to do so.

(6) The Lord Chief Justice must consult the Lord Chancellor before making a nomination under this paragraph.

Appeals

4 (1) Where –

(a) by virtue of this Schedule an investigation is conducted by a person who holds or has held office as a judge of the High Court (including the Chief Coroner if he or she is such a person) or by a person who has held office as a judge of the Court of Appeal, and
(b) the investigation gives rise to an appeal under section 40,

that section has effect as if references in it to the Chief Coroner were references to the Court of Appeal, and with the omission of subsections (8) and (9).

(2) Where –

(a) by virtue of this Schedule an investigation is conducted by a Circuit judge (including the Chief Coroner if he or she is a Circuit judge), and
(b) the investigation gives rise to an appeal under section 40,

that section has effect as if references in it to the Chief Coroner were references to a judge of the High Court nominated by the Lord Chief Justice.

Investigations already begun

5 A reference in this Schedule to conducting an investigation, in the case of an investigation that has already begun, is to be read as a reference to continuing to conduct the investigation.

SCHEDULE 11 AMENDMENTS TO THE CORONERS ACT (NORTHERN IRELAND) 1959

(Section 49)

Witnesses and evidence

1 In the Coroners Act (Northern Ireland) 1959, for section 17 (witnesses to be summoned) substitute –

'17A Power to require evidence to be given or produced

(1) A coroner who proceeds to hold an inquest may by notice require a person to attend at a time and place stated in the notice and –

(a) to give evidence at the inquest,
(b) to produce any documents in the custody or under the control of the person which relate to a matter that is relevant to the inquest, or
(c) to produce for inspection, examination or testing any other thing in the custody or under the control of the person which relates to a matter that is relevant to the inquest.

(2) A coroner who is making any investigation to determine whether or not an inquest is necessary, or who proceeds to hold an inquest, may by notice require a person, within such period as the coroner thinks reasonable –

(a) to provide evidence to the coroner, about any matters specified in the notice, in the form of a written statement,
(b) to produce any documents in the custody or under the control of the person which relate to a matter that is relevant to the investigation or inquest, or
(c) to produce for inspection, examination or testing any other thing in the custody or under the control of the person which relates to a matter that is relevant to the investigation or inquest.

(3) A notice under subsection (1) or (2) shall –

(a) explain the possible consequences, under subsection (6), of not complying with the notice;

(b) indicate what the recipient of the notice should do if he wishes to make a claim under subsection (4).

(4) A claim by a person that –

(a) he is unable to comply with a notice under this section, or
(b) it is not reasonable in all the circumstances to require him to comply with such a notice,

is to be determined by the coroner, who may revoke or vary the notice on that ground.

(5) In deciding whether to revoke or vary a notice on the ground mentioned in subsection (4)(b), the coroner shall consider the public interest in the information in question being obtained for the purposes of the inquest, having regard to the likely importance of the information.

(6) A coroner may impose a fine not exceeding £1000 on a person who fails without reasonable excuse to do anything required by a notice under subsection (1) or (2).

(7) For the purposes of this section a document or thing is under a person's control if it is in the person's possession or if he has a right to possession of it.

(8) Nothing in this section shall prevent a person who has not been given a notice under subsection (1) or (2) from giving or producing any evidence, document or other thing.

17B Giving or producing evidence: further provision

(1) The power of a coroner under section 17A(6) is additional to, and does not affect, any other power the coroner may have –

(a) to compel a person to appear before him;
(b) to compel a person to give evidence or produce any document or other thing;
(c) to punish a person for contempt of court for failure to appear or to give evidence or to produce any document or other thing.

But a person may not be fined under that section and also be punished under any such other power.

(2) A person may not be required to give or produce any evidence or document under section 17A if –

(a) he could not be required to do so in civil proceedings in a court in Northern Ireland, or
(b) the requirement would be incompatible with a Community obligation.

(3) The rules of law under which evidence or documents are permitted or required to be withheld on grounds of public interest immunity apply in relation to an inquest as they apply in relation to civil proceedings in a court in Northern Ireland.

17C Offences relating to evidence

(1) It is an offence for a person to do anything that is intended to have the effect of –

(a) distorting or otherwise altering any evidence, document or other thing that is given or produced for the purposes of any investigation or inquest under this Act, or
(b) preventing any evidence, document or other thing from being given or produced for the purposes of such an investigation or inquest,

or to do anything that the person knows or believes is likely to have that effect.

(2) It is an offence for a person –

(a) intentionally to suppress or conceal a document that is, and that the person knows or believes to be, a relevant document, or
(b) intentionally to alter or destroy such a document.

(3) For the purposes of subsection (2) a document is a "relevant document" if it is likely that a coroner making any investigation or holding an inquest would (if aware of its existence) wish to be provided with it.
(4) A person does not commit an offence under subsection (1) or (2) by doing anything that is authorised or required –

(a) by a coroner, or
(b) by virtue of section 17B(2) or (3) or any privilege that applies.

(5) Proceedings for an offence under subsection (1) or (2) may be instituted only by or with the consent of the Director of Public Prosecutions for Northern Ireland.
(6) A person guilty of an offence under subsection (1) or (2) is liable on summary conviction to a fine not exceeding level 3 on the standard scale, or to imprisonment for a term not exceeding 6 months, or to both.'

2 Omit sections 19 (service of summonses) and 20 (provisions as to witnesses) of that Act.

ooo

SCHEDULE 21 MINOR AND CONSEQUENTIAL AMENDMENTS

(Section 177)

PART 1 CORONERS ETC

Cremation Act 1902

1 In section 10 of the Cremation Act 1902 (saving for coroners), for 'the Coroners Act 1988' substitute 'Part 1 of the Coroners and Justice Act 2009'.

Births and Deaths Registration Act 1926

2 The Births and Deaths Registration Act 1926 is amended as follows.
3 In section 4 (prohibition of removal of body out of England without notice), for 'the coroner within whose jurisdiction the body is lying' substitute 'the senior coroner in whose area the body is situated,'.
4 In section 5 (burial of still-born children), for the words after 'delivered to him' substitute 'either –

(a) a certificate given by the registrar under section 11(2) or (3) of the Births and Deaths Registration Act 1953, or
(b) in a case in relation to which a senior coroner has made enquiries under section 1(7) of the Coroners and Justice Act 2009 (or has purported to conduct an investigation under Part 1 of that Act), an order of the coroner.'

Visiting Forces Act 1952

5 (1) Section 7 of the Visiting Forces Act 1952 (provisions as to coroners' inquests etc) is amended as follows.
(2) For subsection (1) substitute –

'(1) Subsections (1A) and (1B) of this section apply if a coroner who has jurisdiction to conduct an investigation under Part 1 of the Coroners and Justice Act 2009 into a person's death is satisfied that the deceased person, at the time of the death, had a relevant association with a visiting force.

(1A) If no investigation into the person's death has begun, the coroner shall not begin an investigation unless directed to do so by the Lord Chancellor.

(1B) If an investigation into the person's death has begun but has not been completed, the coroner shall suspend the investigation unless directed not to do so by the Lord Chancellor.'

(3) In subsection (2) –

(a) for the words from 'the last' to 'a death' substitute 'subsections (1) to (1B) of this section, if in the course of an investigation under Part 1 of the Coroners and Justice Act 2009 into a person's death',
(b) for 'Secretary of State' substitute 'Lord Chancellor',
(c) for the words from 'adjourn the inquest' to 'discharge the jury,' substitute 'suspend the investigation', and
(d) for 'at the inquest' substitute 'in the course of the investigation'.

(4) After subsection (2) insert –

'(2A) A coroner who suspends an investigation under this section shall –

(a) adjourn any inquest being held as part of the investigation, and
(b) discharge any jury that has been summoned.

(2B) The suspension of an investigation under this section does not prevent its suspension under Schedule 1 to the Coroners and Justice Act 2009; and vice versa.'

(5) For subsection (3) substitute –

'(3) Where an investigation is suspended under this section, the coroner shall not resume it except on the direction of the Lord Chancellor.

(3A) Where the investigation is resumed, the coroner must resume any inquest that was adjourned under subsection (2A).

(3B) A resumed inquest may be held with a jury if the coroner thinks that there is sufficient reason for it to be held with one.'

(6) In subsection (4), for the words from 'the Secretary of State' to 'to be held' substitute 'the Lord Chancellor under subsection (1A) or (3) of this section, an investigation is required to be conducted'.

(7) In subsection (5), for 'section two of the said Act of 1926' substitute 'section 24 of the Births and Deaths Registration Act 1953'.

(8) For subsection (7) substitute –

'(7) In the application of this section to Northern Ireland –

(a) in subsection (1), for "a coroner who has jurisdiction to conduct an investigation under Part 1 of the Coroners and Justice Act 2009 into a person's death" there is substituted "a coroner who has jurisdiction under the Coroners Act (Northern Ireland) 1959 to hold an inquest into a person's death";
(b) in subsection (1A), for "no investigation" there is substituted "no inquest" and for "an investigation" there is substituted "an inquest";
(c) in subsection (1B), for "an investigation" there is substituted "an inquest", and for "suspend the investigation" there is substituted "adjourn the inquest";

(d) in subsection (2) –
(i) for "in the course of an investigation under Part 1 of the Coroners and Justice Act 2009" there is substituted "on an inquest";
(ii) for "suspend the investigation" there is substituted "adjourn the inquest";
(iii) for "in the course of the investigation" there is substituted "at the inquest";
(e) in subsection (2A), for the words from "suspends an investigation" to the end there is substituted "adjourns an inquest under this section shall discharge any jury that has been summoned";
(f) in subsection (3), for "investigation is suspended" there is substituted "inquest is adjourned";
(g) subsection (3A) is omitted;
(h) in subsection (3B), for "A resumed inquest" there is substituted "An inquest resumed under this section";
(i) subsections (4) and (5) are omitted.'

Births and Deaths Registration Act 1953

6 The Births and Deaths Registration Act 1953 is amended as follows.

7 In section 2 (information concerning birth to be given to registrar within 42 days), in paragraph (ii) of the proviso, for 'an inquest is held at which' substitute 'an investigation is conducted under Part 1 of the 2009 Act, other than one that is discontinued under section 4 of that Act (cause of death revealed by post-mortem examination), in the course of which'.

8 (1) Section 16 (information concerning death in a house) is amended as follows.
(2) In subsection (2) –
(a) in paragraph (a), for 'any relative of the deceased person' substitute 'any person who is a relative or the partner of the deceased and who was',
(b) in paragraph (b), for 'any other relative of the deceased residing or being' substitute 'any person who is a relative or the partner of the deceased and who is or resides', and
(c) after paragraph (b) insert –

'(ba) any personal representative of the deceased;'.

(3) In subsection (3) –
(a) in paragraph (a), for 'the nearest relative such' substitute 'each such person',
(b) in paragraph (b) –
(i) for 'no such relative' substitute 'no such person', and
(ii) for 'each such relative' substitute 'each such person',
(c) in paragraph (c) –
(i) for 'if there are no such relatives' substitute 'if neither of paragraphs (a) and (b) above applies', and
(ii) for 'paragraph (c) or (d)' substitute 'paragraph (ba), (c) or (d)',
(d) in paragraph (d), for 'if there are no such relatives or persons as aforesaid' substitute 'if none of paragraphs (a) to (c) above applies', and
(e) for 'five days from the date of the death' substitute 'five days from the relevant date'.

(4) In that subsection, for paragraph (ii) of the proviso substitute –

'(ii) this subsection shall not have effect if an investigation is conducted under Part 1 of the 2009 Act into the death of the deceased person and has not been discontinued under section 4 of that Act (cause of death revealed by post-mortem examination).'

(5) After that subsection insert –

'(4) In this section, the expression "the relevant date" means –

(a) the date on which the registrar is notified in accordance with regulations under section 20(1)(f)(i) or (h)(i) of the 2009 Act (confirmation or certification by medical examiner of cause of death); or

(b) where an investigation under Part 1 of that Act into the death of the deceased person is discontinued under section 4 of that Act, the date of the discontinuance.'

9 (1) Section 17 (information concerning other deaths) is amended as follows.

(2) In subsection (2) –

(a) in paragraph (a), for 'any relative of the deceased who' substitute 'any person who is a relative or the partner of the deceased and who', and

(b) after that paragraph insert –

'(aa) any personal representative of the deceased;'.

(3) In subsection (3) –

(a) in paragraph (a), for 'relative' substitute 'person',

(b) in paragraph (b), for 'relatives' substitute 'persons',

(c) for 'five days from the date of the death or of the finding of the body' substitute 'five days from the relevant date', and

(d) for paragraph (ii) of the proviso substitute –

'(ii) this subsection shall not have effect if an investigation is conducted under Part 1 of the 2009 Act into the death of the deceased person and has not been discontinued under section 4 of that Act (cause of death revealed by post-mortem examination).'

(4) After that subsection insert –

'(4) In this section, the expression "the relevant date" means –

(a) the date on which the registrar is notified in accordance with regulations under section 20(1)(f)(i) or (h)(i) of the 2009 Act (confirmation or certification by medical examiner of cause of death); or

(b) where an investigation under Part 1 of that Act into the death of the deceased person is discontinued under section 4 of that Act, the date of the discontinuance.'

10 (1) Section 18 (notice preliminary to information of death) is amended as follows.

(2) For the words from the beginning to 'that person's death' substitute 'If, before the expiration of five days from the relevant date, a qualified informant of a person's death'.

(3) For the words from 'accompanied by a notice' to 'the cause of death,' substitute 'accompanied by a confirmed attending practitioner's certificate, or a medical examiner's certificate issued in accordance with regulations under section 20 of the 2009 Act (medical certificate of cause of death),'.

(4) For 'from the date aforesaid' substitute 'from the relevant date'.

(5) At the end of that section (which becomes subsection (1)) insert –

'(2) In this section, the expression "the relevant date" means –

(a) the date on which the registrar is notified in accordance with regulations under section 20(1)(f)(i) or (h)(i) of the 2009 Act (confirmation or certification by medical examiner of cause of death); or

(b) where an investigation under Part 1 of that Act into the death of the deceased person is discontinued under section 4 of that Act (cause of death revealed by post-mortem examination), the date of the discontinuance.'

11 (1) In section 19 (registrar's power to require information concerning death), subsection (1) is amended as follows.

(2) For the words from the beginning to 'the registrar may' substitute –

'(A1) This section applies where, after the expiration of the relevant period from –

(a) the date on which the registrar is notified in accordance with regulations under section 20(1)(f)(i) or (h)(i) of the 2009 Act (confirmation or certification by medical examiner of cause of death), or

(b) where an investigation under Part 1 of that Act into a person's death is discontinued under section 4 of that Act (cause of death revealed by post-mortem examination), the date of the discontinuance,

the death of that person has, owing to the default of the persons required to give information concerning it, not been registered.

(1) The registrar may'.

(3) For paragraph (ii) of the proviso substitute –

'(ii) an investigation under Part 1 of the 2009 Act is conducted into the death of the deceased person and has not been discontinued under section 4 of that Act'.

12 In section 20 (registration of death free of charge) omit the words from ', at any time' to 'of any person,'.

13 Omit section 21 (registration of death after twelve months).

14 For section 22 substitute –

'22 Registration of cause of death on receipt of medical certificate

(1) This section applies where –

(a) the registrar is given a confirmed attending practitioner's certificate, or a medical examiner's certificate, in accordance with regulations under section 20 of the 2009 Act (medical certificate of cause of death); and

(b) no investigation into the death under Part 1 of that Act is conducted.

(2) The registrar shall enter in the register the cause of death as stated in the certificate, together with –

(a) the name of the medical examiner and such information about the examiner as may be prescribed; and

(b) where an attending practitioner's certificate was prepared, the name of the practitioner by whom it was prepared and such information about that practitioner as may be prescribed.'

15 (1) Section 23 (furnishing of information by coroner) is amended as follows.

(2) For subsection (2) substitute –

'(2) Where there has been an investigation under Part 1 of the 2009 Act into a death and the senior coroner sends to the registrar a certificate giving information concerning the death, including the particulars found under section 10(1)(b) of that Act, the registrar shall in the prescribed form and manner register the death and those particulars; and, if the death has been previously registered, those particulars shall be entered in the prescribed manner without any alteration of the original entry.

(2ZA) Where under section 40(8)(a)(i) of the 2009 Act the Chief Coroner amends a finding under section 10(1)(b) of that Act and sends to the registrar a certificate setting out the amended particulars, the registrar shall in the prescribed form and manner register the amended particulars without any alteration of the original entry.'

(3) For subsection (2A) substitute –

'(2A) Where –

(a) an investigation under Part 1 of the 2009 Act into a death is suspended under Schedule 1 to that Act, and
(b) the senior coroner sends to the registrar a certificate stating the particulars required by this Act to be registered concerning the death (so far as they have been ascertained at the date of the certificate),

the registrar shall in the prescribed form and manner register the death and those particulars.

(2B) Where –

(a) an investigation under Part 1 of the 2009 Act into a death is suspended under paragraph 2 of Schedule 1 to that Act (suspension where certain criminal proceedings brought), and
(b) the senior coroner sends to the registrar a certificate –
(i) stating the result of the proceedings in respect of the charge or charges by reason of which the investigation was suspended, or of any proceedings that had to be concluded before the investigation could be resumed, or
(ii) setting out any changes or additions to the particulars mentioned in subsection (2A) of this section,

the registrar shall in the prescribed form and manner register the result of those proceedings, or the changes or additions, without any alteration of the original entry.

(2C) Where –

(a) an investigation under Part 1 of the 2009 Act into a death is suspended under paragraph 3 of Schedule 1 to that Act (suspension pending inquiry), and
(b) the senior coroner sends to the registrar a certificate –
(i) stating the findings of the inquiry by reason of which the investigation was suspended,
(ii) stating the result of any proceedings that had to be concluded before the investigation could be resumed, or
(iii) setting out any changes or additions to the particulars mentioned in subsection (2A) of this section,

the registrar shall in the prescribed form and manner register the findings of that inquiry, or the result of those proceedings, or the changes or additions, without any alteration of the original entry.'

(4) In subsection (3), for the words from the beginning to 'stating' substitute

'Where an investigation is discontinued under section 4 of the 2009 Act by reason of an examination under section 14 of that Act (post-mortem examinations) and the senior coroner sends to the registrar a certificate stating'.

16 (1) Section 23A (giving of information concerning a death to a person other than the registrar) is amended as follows.

(2) In subsection (2), for paragraphs (a) and (b) substitute –

'(a) if there has been no investigation under Part 1 of the 2009 Act into the death, a copy of a confirmed attending practitioner's certificate, or of a medical examiner's certificate, given to the registrar in accordance with regulations under section 20 of the 2009 Act (medical certificate of cause of death); and

(b) if an investigation into the death has been discontinued under section 4 of that Act by reason of an examination under section 14 of that Act (post-mortem examinations), a copy of a certificate from the senior coroner stating the cause of death as disclosed by the report of the person making the examination;'.

(3) In subsection (5), after 'a relative' insert 'or the partner'.

(4) Omit subsection (6).

17 In section 24 (certificates as to registration of death), in subsection (1), for 'has received a certificate under section twenty-two of this Act' substitute 'has been given a confirmed attending practitioner's certificate or a medical examiner's certificate in accordance with regulations under section 20 of the 2009 Act'.

18 (1) Section 29 (correction of error in registers) is amended as follows.

(2) After subsection (3) insert –

'(3A) In the case of a death in relation to which the registrar has been given a confirmed attending practitioner's certificate, or a medical examiner's certificate, in accordance with regulations under section 20 of the 2009 Act –

(a) no correction under subsection (3) of this section relating to the cause of death may be made without the approval of the medical examiner concerned;

(b) any error of fact or substance relating to the cause of death in a register of deaths may be corrected by entry in the margin (without any alteration of the original entry) by the officer having the custody of the register on being notified by the medical examiner of the nature of the error and the true facts of the case.

(3B) In the case of a death in relation to which an investigation under Part 1 of the 2009 Act has been discontinued under section 4 of that Act (cause of death revealed by post-mortem examination) –

(a) no correction under subsection (3) of this section relating to the cause of death may be made without the approval of the senior coroner concerned;

(b) any error of fact or substance relating to the cause of death in a register of deaths may be corrected by entry in the margin (without any alteration of the original entry) by the officer having the custody of the register on being notified by the senior coroner of the nature of the error and the true facts of the case.'

(3) In paragraph (a) of subsection (4), for 'touching which he has held an inquest' substitute 'into which he has conducted an investigation under Part 1 of the 2009 Act (other than one that has been discontinued under section 4 of that Act)'.

(4) Omit paragraph (b) of that subsection and the word 'or' preceding it.

19 After section 33 insert –

'33A Short certificate of death

(1) Any person shall –

(a) on furnishing the prescribed particulars, and
(b) on payment of such fee as may be specified in regulations made by the Minister by statutory instrument,

be entitled to obtain from the Registrar General, a superintendent registrar or a registrar a short certificate of the death of any person.

(2) Any such certificate shall be in the prescribed form and shall be compiled in the prescribed manner from the records and registers in the custody of the Registrar General, or from the registers in the custody of the superintendent registrar or registrar, as the case may be, and shall contain such particulars as may be prescribed.

(3) A statutory instrument containing regulations under subsection (1)(b) of this section shall be subject to annulment in pursuance of a resolution of either House of Parliament.'

20 In section 34 (entry in register as evidence of birth or death) omit subsection (4).

21 (1) In section 41 (interpretation) insert the following definitions at the appropriate places –

'"the 2009 Act" means the Coroners and Justice Act 2009;';

'"attending practitioner's certificate" has the meaning given by section 20(1)(a) of the 2009 Act;';

'"confirmed attending practitioner's certificate" means an attending practitioner's certificate in respect of which the cause of death has been confirmed by a medical examiner in accordance with regulations under section 20(1)(f)(i) of the 2009 Act;';

'"medical examiner" means a person appointed under section 19 of the 2009 Act;';

'"medical examiner's certificate" has the meaning given by section 20(1)(h) of the 2009 Act;';

'"partner" (except in the expression "civil partner") is to be read in accordance with subsection (2) of this section.'

(2) At the end of that section (which becomes subsection (1)) insert –

'(2) A person is the partner of a deceased person if the two of them (whether of different sexes or the same sex) were living as partners in an enduring relationship at the time of the deceased person's death.

(3) A reference in this Act to an investigation under Part 1 of the 2009 Act being conducted includes a reference to the case where such an investigation has begun and –

(a) has not yet finished,
(b) is suspended under Schedule 1 to that Act (whether temporarily or otherwise), or
(c) is discontinued under section 4 of that Act.'

Courts Act 1971

22 In Schedule 2 to the Courts Act 1971 (certain office-holders eligible for appointment as circuit judges), in Part 1A, for 'Coroner appointed under section 2 of the Coroners Act 1988' substitute 'Senior coroner appointed under paragraph 1 of Schedule 3 to the Coroners and Justice Act 2009'.

Pensions (Increase) Act 1971

23 In Schedule 2 to the Pensions (Increase) Act 1971 (official pensions), in paragraph 61, after 'the Coroners Act 1988' insert 'or by virtue of paragraph 17 of Schedule 3 to the Coroners and Justice Act 2009'.

Juries Act 1974

24 In section 19 of the Juries Act 1974 (payment for jury service), in subsections (2) and (5), for 'the Coroners Act 1988' substitute 'Schedule 7 to the Coroners and Justice Act 2009'.

Health and Safety at Work etc. Act 1974

25 (1) In section 34 of the Health and Safety at Work etc. Act 1974 (extension of time for bringing summary proceedings), subsection (1) is amended as follows.

(2) In paragraph (c), for 'a coroner's inquest is held touching' substitute 'an investigation under Part 1 of the Coroners and Justice Act 2009 is conducted into'.

(3) For the words from 'from the report' to 'proceedings at the inquest or' substitute 'from the report or investigation or, in a case falling within paragraph (d) above, from the proceedings at the'.

(4) For 'report, inquest or inquiry' substitute 'report, investigation or inquiry'.

(5) For 'conclusion of the inquest' substitute 'conclusion of the investigation'.

House of Commons Disqualification Act 1975

26 In Part 3 of Schedule 1 to the House of Commons Disqualification Act 1975 (other disqualifying offices) insert the following entries at the appropriate place –

'Senior coroner, area coroner or assistant coroner appointed under Part 1 of the Coroners and Justice Act 2009.'

'Coroner for Treasure.'

'Deputy Chief Coroner appointed by the Lord Chancellor under that Part who is not also a senior coroner.'

Northern Ireland Assembly Disqualification Act 1975

27 In Part 3 of Schedule 1 to the Northern Ireland Assembly Disqualification Act 1975 (other disqualifying offices) insert the following entries at the appropriate place –

'Senior coroner, area coroner or assistant coroner appointed under Part 1 of the Coroners and Justice Act 2009.'

'Coroner for Treasure.'

'Deputy Chief Coroner appointed by the Lord Chancellor under that Part who is not also a senior coroner.'

Magistrates' Courts Act 1980

28 In Schedule 6A to the Magistrates' Courts Act 1980 (fines that may be altered under section 143) –

(a) omit the entry relating to the Coroners Act 1988, and
(b) after the entry relating to the Powers of Criminal Courts (Sentencing) Act 2000 insert –

'CORONERS AND JUSTICE ACT 2009 In Schedule 6, paragraphs 5 (refusal to serve as juror etc) and 6 (refusal to give evidence etc)	£1,000'.

Access to Health Records Act 1990

29 (1) Section 3 of the Access to Health Records Act 1990 (right of access to health records) is amended as follows.

(2) In subsection (1) (persons entitled to access), at the end insert –

'(g) where the patient has died, a medical examiner exercising functions by virtue of section 20 of the Coroners and Justice Act 2009 in relation to the death.'

(3) In subsection (4) (fee for access), at the end insert –

'Paragraphs (a) and (b) above do not apply in the case of access for which an application is made under subsection (1)(g) above.'

Courts and Legal Services Act 1990

30 In Schedule 11 to the Courts and Legal Services Act 1990 (judges etc barred from legal practice), for 'Coroner appointed under section 2 of the Coroners Act 1988' substitute 'Senior coroner appointed under paragraph 1 of Schedule 3 to the Coroners and Justice Act 2009'.

Judicial Pensions and Retirement Act 1993

31 In Part 2 of Schedule 1 to the Judicial Pensions and Retirement Act 1993 (other offices that may be qualifying judicial offices), after the entry relating to the Adjudicator to Her Majesty's Land Registry there is inserted –

'Coroner for Treasure.

Deputy Chief Coroner appointed by the Lord Chancellor who is not also a senior coroner.'

Merchant Shipping Act 1995

32 The Merchant Shipping Act 1995 is amended as follows.

33 In section 108 (returns of births and deaths in ships etc), in subsection (6)(b), for 'is satisfied that an inquest is unnecessary' substitute 'discontinues an investigation under Part 1 of the Coroners and Justice Act 2009 or, as the case may be, is satisfied that an inquest under the Coroners Act (Northern Ireland) 1959 is unnecessary'.

34 In section 271 (inquiries into deaths of crew members and others), in subsection (6), for 'where' to the end substitute 'where –

(a) in England and Wales, an investigation is to be conducted under Part 1 of the Coroners and Justice Act 2009;

(b) in Northern Ireland, an inquest is to be held under the Coroners Act (Northern Ireland) 1959;

(c) in Scotland, an enquiry is to be held under the Fatal Accidents and Sudden Deaths Inquiry (Scotland) Act 1976.'

35 (1) Section 273 (transmission of particulars of certain deaths on ships) is amended as follows.

(2) In paragraph (a), for 'or a post mortem examination' to the end substitute 'or subsection (2) below applies; and'.

(3) At the end of that section (which becomes subsection (1)) insert –

'(2) This subsection applies where –

(a) in England and Wales, an investigation under Part 1 of the Coroners and Justice Act 2009 into a person's death is discontinued under section 4 of that Act (cause of death revealed by post-mortem examination); or

(b) in Northern Ireland, a preliminary investigation is made of a dead body as a result of which the coroner is satisfied that an inquest is unnecessary.'

Employment Rights Act 1996

36 (1) The Employment Rights Act 1996 is amended as follows.

(2) In section 43M (jury service), in subsection (1)(a), for 'the Coroners Act 1988' substitute 'Part 1 of the Coroners and Justice Act 2009'.

(3) In section 98B (jury service), in subsection (1)(a), for 'the Coroners Act 1988' substitute 'Part 1 of the Coroners and Justice Act 2009'.

Treasure Act 1996

37 The Treasure Act 1996 is amended as follows.

38 For section 7 (jurisdiction of coroners) substitute –

'7 Jurisdiction of coroners

(1) As regards Northern Ireland, the jurisdiction of coroners which is referred to in section 33 of the Coroners Act (Northern Ireland) 1959 (treasure) is exercisable in relation to anything that is treasure for the purposes of this Act.

(2) That jurisdiction is not exercisable for the purposes of the law relating to treasure trove in relation to anything found after the commencement of section 4.

(3) The Act of 1959 has effect subject to this section.

(4) An inquest held by virtue of subsection (1) is to be held without a jury, unless the coroner orders otherwise.

(5) As regards England and Wales, see Chapter 4 of Part 1 of the Coroners and Justice Act 2009 (which confers jurisdiction on the Coroner for Treasure in relation to an object that is or may be treasure, or treasure trove found before the commencement of section 4).'

39 (1) Section 8 (duty of finder to notify coroner) is amended as follows.

(2) In subsection (1), for 'coroner for the district in which the object was found' substitute 'Coroner for Treasure'.

(3) In subsection (4), for 'coroner' substitute 'Coroner for Treasure'.

(4) For subsection (5) substitute –

'(5) If the office of Coroner for Treasure is vacant, notification under subsection (1) must be given to an Assistant Coroner for Treasure.

(6) This section has effect subject to section 8B.'

(5) After that subsection insert –

'(7) In its application to Northern Ireland this section has effect as if –

(a) in subsection (1), for "Coroner for Treasure" there were substituted "coroner for the district in which the object was found";
(b) in subsection (4), for "Coroner for Treasure" there were substituted "coroner"; and
(c) in subsection (5), for the words from "Coroner for Treasure" to the end there were substituted "coroner for a district is vacant, the person acting as coroner for that district is the coroner for the purposes of subsection (1).'

40 After section 8A (inserted by section 30 of this Act) insert –

'8B Notice under section 8 or 8A to designated officer

(1) A requirement under section 8 or 8A to give a notification to the Coroner for Treasure (or an Assistant Coroner for Treasure) may, if the relevant place falls within an area for which there is a designated officer, be complied with by giving the notification to that officer.
(2) A designated officer must notify the Coroner for Treasure of all notifications given under subsection (1).
(3) If the office of Coroner for Treasure is vacant, notification under subsection (2) must be given to an Assistant Coroner for Treasure.
(4) In this section –

"designated officer" means an officer designated by an order made by statutory instrument by the Secretary of State;

"the relevant place" means –

(a) in relation to a requirement under section 8, the place where the object in question was found;
(b) in relation to a requirement under section 8A, the place where the treasure in question is located.

(5) A statutory instrument containing an order under this section shall be subject to annulment in pursuance of a resolution of either House of Parliament.
(6) In its application to Northern Ireland this section has effect as if –

(a) in subsection (1), for "the Coroner for Treasure (or an Assistant Coroner for Treasure)" there were substituted "a coroner";
(b) in subsection (2), for "Coroner for Treasure" there were substituted "coroner for the district in which the relevant place falls";
(c) in subsection (3), for the words from "Coroner for Treasure" to "Assistant Coroner for Treasure" there were substituted "coroner for a district is vacant, the person acting as coroner for that district is the coroner for the purposes of subsection (2)".

8C Offences under section 8 or 8A: period for bringing proceedings

(1) Proceedings for an offence under section 8 or 8A may be brought within the period of six months from the date on which evidence sufficient in the opinion of the prosecutor to warrant the proceedings came to the prosecutor's knowledge; but no such proceedings may be brought by virtue of this subsection more than three years after the commission of the offence.
(2) For the purposes of subsection (1) –

(a) a certificate signed by or on behalf of the prosecutor and stating the date on which the evidence referred to in that subsection came to the prosecutor's knowledge shall be conclusive evidence to that effect; and

(b) a certificate to that effect and purporting to be so signed shall be deemed to be so signed unless the contrary is proved.'

41 For section 9 substitute –

'9 Procedure for investigations: England and Wales

(1) Before conducting an investigation concerning an object, the Coroner for Treasure must –

(a) notify the appropriate national museum;
(b) take reasonable steps to notify –

(i) any person who the coroner thinks may have found the object; and
(ii) any person who, at the time the object was found, occupied land that the coroner thinks may be where it was found.

(2) During an investigation the Coroner for Treasure must take reasonable steps to notify any person within subsection (1)(b) who has not already been notified.

(3) Before or during an investigation, the Coroner for Treasure must take reasonable steps –

(a) to obtain the names and addresses of any other interested persons; and
(b) to notify any interested person whose name and address he obtains.

(4) The Coroner for Treasure must take reasonable steps to give any interested person an opportunity to examine witnesses at any inquest held as part of an investigation.

(5) In this section –

"the appropriate national museum" means –

(a) the British Museum, if the object in question was found or is believed to have been found in England;
(b) the National Museum of Wales, if it was found or is believed to have been found in Wales;

"interested person" has the meaning given by section 47(6) of the Coroners and Justice Act 2009;

"investigation" means an investigation under section 26 of that Act.

(6) This section extends only to England and Wales.

9A Procedure for inquests: Northern Ireland

(1) Before conducting an inquest concerning an object, a coroner must –

(a) notify the Department of the Environment for Northern Ireland;
(b) take reasonable steps to notify –

(i) any person who the coroner thinks may have found the object; and
(ii) any person who, at the time the object was found, occupied land that the coroner thinks may be where it was found.

(2) During the inquest the coroner must take reasonable steps to notify any person within subsection (1)(b) who has not already been notified.

(3) Before or during the inquest, the coroner must take reasonable steps –

(a) to obtain the names and addresses of any other interested persons; and
(b) to notify any interested person whose name and address he obtains.

(4) The coroner must take reasonable steps to give any interested person an opportunity to examine witnesses at the inquest.
(5) In this section –

"inquest" means an inquest held by virtue of section 7(1);

"interested person" means –

(a) the Department of the Environment for Northern Ireland;
(b) the finder of the object in question or any person otherwise involved in the find;
(c) the occupier, at the time the object was found, of the land where it was found or is believed to have been found;
(d) a person who had an interest in that land at that time or who has had such an interest since;
(e) any other person with a sufficient interest.

(6) This section extends only to Northern Ireland.'

42 Omit section 13.

Northern Ireland (Location of Victims' Remains) Act 1999

43 In section 4 of the Northern Ireland (Location of Victims' Remains) Act 1999 (restrictions on forensic testing), in subsection (2), for 'for the purposes of an inquest, the identity' substitute

'for the purposes of –

(a) an inquest under the Coroners Act (Northern Ireland) 1959, or
(b) an investigation under Part 1 of the Coroners and Justice Act 2009,

the identity'.

Freedom of Information Act 2000

44 In section 32 of the Freedom of Information Act 2000 (court records etc), in subsection (4)(b), for 'any inquest or' substitute 'any investigation under Part 1 of the Coroners and Justice Act 2009, any inquest under the Coroners Act (Northern Ireland) 1959 and any'.

International Criminal Court Act 2001

45 In section 35 of the International Criminal Court Act 2001 (orders for exhumation), for 'section 23 of the Coroners Act 1988' substitute 'paragraph 6 of Schedule 5 to the Coroners and Justice Act 2009'.

Courts Act 2003

46 In Schedule 3A to the Courts Act 2003 (further provision about the inspectors of court administration), in paragraph 2(2) (inspection programmes and inspection frameworks: consultation etc), after 'the Lord Chief Justice of England and Wales' insert ', the Chief Coroner'.

Human Tissue Act 2004

47 The Human Tissue Act 2004 is amended as follows.
48 In section 1 (authorisation of activities for scheduled purposes), in subsection (2), for the words after 'shall be lawful' substitute

'if done with the appropriate consent and after –

(a) the confirmation of the cause of death by a medical examiner in accordance with regulations under section 20(1)(f)(i) of the Coroners and Justice Act 2009 or the issue by a medical examiner of a certificate of the cause of death in accordance with regulations under section 20(1)(h)(i) of that Act, or

(b) the signing of a certificate under Article 25(2) of the Births and Deaths Registration (Northern Ireland) Order 1976 of the cause of the person's death.'

49 (1) Section 5 (prohibition of activities without consent etc) is amended as follows.

(2) In subsection (3), for the words from 'neither' to the end substitute

'none of the following has happened in relation to the death of the person concerned –

(a) the confirmation of the cause of death by a medical examiner in accordance with regulations under section 20(1)(f)(i) of the Coroners and Justice Act 2009 or the issue by a medical examiner of a certificate of the cause of death in accordance with regulations under section 20(1)(h)(i) of that Act;

(b) the signing of a certificate under Article 25(2) of the Births and Deaths Registration (Northern Ireland) Order 1976 of the cause of death.'

(3) In subsection (4)(a)(i), for 'a certificate under either of those provisions has been signed in relation to the cause of death of the person concerned' substitute 'one of the things mentioned in paragraphs (a) and (b) of that subsection has happened in relation to the death of the person concerned'.

50 In section 43 (preservation for transplantation), after subsection (5) insert –

'(5A) Section 11(2) applies to an act on authority under subsection (1) above as it applies to an act on authority under section 1.'

Constitutional Reform Act 2005

51 In Schedule 14 to the Constitutional Reform Act 2005 (the Judicial Appointments Commission: relevant offices and enactments), at the end of Part 3 insert –

'Coroner for Treasure	Paragraph 1 of Schedule 4 to the Coroners and Justice Act 2009
Deputy Chief Coroner	Paragraph 2(5) to Schedule 8 of the Coroners and Justice Act 2009'

ooo

SCHEDULE 22 TRANSITIONAL, TRANSITORY AND SAVING PROVISIONS (SECTION 177)

PART 1 CORONERS ETC

Coroner areas

1 (1) Where an order is made under section 182(4) bringing into force the repeal of sections 1 to 7 of the 1988 Act (coroners, coroners' districts and deputy coroners), the Lord Chancellor must make an order under paragraph 1 of Schedule 2 –

(a) specifying as a coroner area the area of each coroner's district immediately before the repeal, and
(b) coming into force at the same time as the repeal.

The order made by virtue of this sub-paragraph is referred to in this Schedule as the 'transitional order'.

(2) Paragraph 1(2) of Schedule 2 does not apply to the coroner areas specified in the transitional order.
(3) The transitional order must specify, as the name of each coroner area, the name by which the corresponding coroner's district was known (but ending 'coroner area' instead of 'coroner's district').
(4) The transitional order must, in relation to each coroner area, contain the provision that may be made under paragraph 2(1)(b) of Schedule 3 (minimum number of assistant coroners).

Relevant authorities

2 (1) For the purposes of this Part, the 'relevant authority' for each coroner area specified in the transitional order is the authority that was the relevant council under the 1988 Act for the corresponding coroner's district.
(2) This paragraph does not apply in relation to a coroner area specified in any subsequent order under Schedule 2.

Senior and assistant coroners

3 (1) Sub-paragraphs (2) and (3) apply on the coming into force of the repeal by this Act of sections 1 to 7 of the 1988 Act.
(2) A person who –

(a) immediately before the repeal was the coroner for a district, and
(b) would, but for the repeal, continue in office,

is to be treated as having been appointed under paragraph 1(1) of Schedule 3 as the senior coroner for the corresponding coroner area.

(3) A person who –

(a) immediately before the repeal was the deputy coroner or an assistant deputy coroner appointed by the coroner for a district, and
(b) would, but for the repeal, continue in office,

is to be treated as having been appointed under paragraph 2(4) of Schedule 3 as an assistant coroner for the corresponding coroner area.

(4) A person who –

(a) becomes an assistant coroner as the result of sub-paragraph (3), and
(b) would accordingly (but for this sub-paragraph) be entitled to fees under paragraph 16 of Schedule 3,

is instead entitled to a salary under paragraph 15 of that Schedule if immediately before becoming an assistant coroner he or she was a deputy coroner remunerated by a salary.

(5) Paragraphs 15(6) and 17 of Schedule 3 have effect as if a reference to an area coroner included a reference to a person within sub-paragraph (4).
(6) Paragraphs 3 and 4 of Schedule 3 do not apply in relation to a deemed appointment under sub-paragraph (2) or (3) above.
(7) Paragraph 10 of that Schedule does not apply to a person who becomes a senior coroner, area coroner or assistant coroner as the result of sub-paragraph (2) or (3) above.
(8) Sub-paragraphs (9) to (11) apply where an order under paragraph 2 of Schedule

2 has the effect of creating a coroner area ('the new area') that consists of or includes some or all of the area of one or more existing coroner areas ('the old areas').

(9) A person who does not meet the criteria in paragraph 3 of Schedule 3, or who falls within paragraph 4 of that Schedule, may nevertheless become the senior coroner or an area coroner for the new area at its inception if he or she is someone who –

(a) was treated by virtue of sub-paragraph (2) above as having been appointed as the senior coroner for one of the old areas, and
(b) held office as such immediately before the inception of the new area.

(10) A person who does not meet the criteria in paragraph 3 of Schedule 3, or who falls within paragraph 4 of that Schedule, may nevertheless become an assistant coroner for the new area at its inception if he or she is someone who –

(a) was treated by virtue of sub-paragraph (2) or (3) above as having been appointed as the senior coroner or an assistant coroner for one of the old areas, and
(b) held office as such immediately before the inception of the new area.

(11) Paragraph 10 of that Schedule does not apply to –

(a) a person within paragraphs (a) and (b) of sub-paragraph (9) above who becomes the senior coroner for the new area at its inception;
(b) a person within paragraphs (a) and (b) of sub-paragraph (10) above who becomes an assistant coroner for the new area at its inception.

Coroner for Treasure

4 In the case of the first appointment to the office of Coroner for Treasure, paragraph 2(b) of Schedule 4 does not apply to a person holding office as a coroner, deputy coroner or assistant deputy coroner under the 1988 Act on the coming into force of that Schedule.

Investigation by former coroner

5 A person who –

(a) was appointed as a coroner under section 1 of the 1988 Act, and
(b) ceased to hold office as such before the coming into force of the repeal by this Act of that section,

is to be treated for the purposes of paragraph 3(3) of Schedule 10 as having held office as a senior coroner.

Interpretation

6 In this Part –

'the 1988 Act' means the Coroners Act 1988;

'coroner's district' or

'district' means a coroner's district for the purposes of the 1988 Act;

'corresponding coroner area', in relation to a district, means the coroner area that (by virtue of the transitional order) has the same area as that district;

'corresponding coroner's district', in relation to a coroner area, means the coroner's district whose area becomes (by virtue of the transitional order) the area of that coroner area;

'transitional order' means the order made by virtue of paragraph 1(1).

ooo

SCHEDULE 23 REPEALS (SECTION 178)

PART 1 CORONERS ETC

Short title and chapter	Extent of repeal
Births and Deaths Registration Act 1953	In section 20, from ', at any time' to 'of any person,'. Section 21. Section 23A(6). In section 29(4), paragraph (b) and the 'or' preceding it. Section 34(4).
Coroners Act (Northern Ireland) 1959	Section 19. Section 20.
Juries Act 1974	Section 22(1).
Magistrates' Courts Act 1980	In Schedule 6A, the entry relating to the Coroners Act 1988.
Coroners Act 1988	The whole Act.
Caldey Island Act 1990	Section 3. In section 4(1), paragraph (c).
Local Government (Wales) Act 1994	In Schedule 17, paragraph 23.
Treasure Act 1996	Section 13.
Access to Justice Act 1999	Section 71. Section 104(1). In Schedule 2, in paragraph 2, the 'and' following paragraph (3).
Regional Assemblies (Preparations) Act 2003	In the Schedule, paragraph 2.
Courts Act 2003	In Schedule 8, paragraph 302.
Criminal Justice Act 2003	In Schedule 3, paragraph 59.
Domestic Violence, Crime and Victims Act 2004	In Schedule 10, paragraphs 26 and 27.
Human Tissue Act 2004	In Schedule 6, paragraph 3.
Constitutional Reform Act 2005	In Schedule 1, paragraphs 19 to 21. In Schedule 4, paragraphs 193 to 195. In Schedule 7, in paragraph 4, the entry in Part A relating to the Coroners Act 1988.
Road Safety Act 2006	Section 20(5). Section 21(4).
Armed Forces Act 2006	In Schedule 16, paragraphs 110 and 111.

Short title and chapter	Extent of repeal
Corporate Manslaughter and Corporate Homicide Act 2007	In Schedule 2, paragraph 1.
Local Government and Public Involvement in Health Act 2007	In Schedule 1, paragraph 15.

°°°

Appendix 2
DRAFT CHARTER FOR BEREAVED PEOPLE

DRAFT CHARTER FOR BEREAVED PEOPLE WHO COME INTO CONTACT WITH A REFORMED CORONER SYSTEM (JANUARY 2009)

1. NB This is a charter for a reformed service, NOT for the service as it is currently structured and currently operates. It is a charter for family members of a person who has died and who a coroner has decided is a 'properly interested person'. At the earliest stages of an investigation – the post-mortem in particular – it will not always be possible for the coroner to have made such a decision, and it will be for the coroner to decide who is to receive information at these stages. Separate information will be prepared for those who are also given interested person status by the coroner, but who are not related to the person who has died.

General

2. A coroner's investigation is required if the death is violent, unnatural, of unknown cause, or occurred while the person is detained by the State.
3. The purposes of the coroner service, when a death is reported to it, are:
   - to establish whether a coroner's investigation is required
   - if so, to establish the identity of someone who has died, and how, when, and where the person died
   - to assist in the prevention of future deaths
   - to provide public reassurance.
4. HM Coroners are independent judicial office holders operating within the legal framework of the Coroners and Justice Act 2009. They are supported by coroner's officers who are employed by either the local police authority or the local authority, and by administrative staff who are employed by the local police authority or the local authority. Together, they comprise the coroner service. This charter sets out the objectives of the service, following reform, and the rights and responsibilities of bereaved people during coronial investigations, including inquests.
5. Most full investigations take between 6 and 12 months to complete, but a small number will take less than this, and an even smaller number of complex cases will take longer.

Definitions

6. 'Inform', or 'informed' means the giving of information by leaflet, letter, e-mail, telephone call, via a website or face to face.
7. 'Working day' means any day between Monday and Friday inclusive, with the exception of Christmas Day, Good Friday or a bank holiday in England and Wales under the Banking and Financial Dealings Act 1971.
8. 'Appropriate next of kin' means the person identified by the coroner or coroner's officer to act as the main contact point to receive information.
9. 'Family member' means a spouse, civil partner, partner, parent, child, brother, sister,

grandparent, grandchild, child of a brother or sister, stepfather, stepmother, half-brother or half-sister of the deceased.

Objectives

10. In a reformed coroner service, the coroner's office will:
    - help bereaved people understand the cause of the death of the person who has died
    - inform bereaved people about the role and powers of the coroner
    - inform bereaved people of their rights and responsibilities if a coroner's investigation is conducted in relation to the death
    - take account, where possible, of individual, family, and community wishes, feelings and expectations, including family and community preferences, traditions and religious requirements relating to mourning and to funerals, and respect for individual and family privacy
    - enable bereaved people, including children and young people where appropriate, to be informed and consulted during the investigation process, treating them with sensitivity, and helping them to find further help where this is necessary
    - answer bereaved people's questions about coronial procedures as promptly and effectively as possible
    - explain, where relevant and on request, why the coroner intends to take no further action in a particular case
    - provide information about how bereaved people may appeal against or complain about the coroner's decisions, and respond to appeals and complaints within the period and in the form specified by the Chief Coroner.

When a death is reported

11. When a death is reported to the coroner, the coroner's office will contact the most appropriate next of kin, where known, and where possible, within 1 working day of the death being reported to explain why the death has been reported and what steps are likely to follow.
12. The appropriate next of kin will be given information as soon as possible, on where they can view the body if they wish to do so and on arrangements for viewing. They will be advised sensitively if the nature of the death may cause the viewing of the body to be particularly distressing.

Right of a family to report a death to the coroner

13. If a family member believes that a doctor, or other relevant professional, has not reported a death to the coroner when they should have done, they may report the death to the coroner personally. This should normally happen before a funeral takes place.
14. The coroner will inform the family member what action he or she proposes to take when reports are made in this way.

Post-mortems

15. Where a coroner orders a post-mortem, the appropriate next of kin will be told by the coroner why it is necessary, when and where it will be performed, and what they should do if they would like to be represented by a doctor at the post-mortem. If the appropriate next of kin, or any other family member, has queries or is unhappy with the decision to hold a post-mortem, they should bring their questions or make known their concerns to the coroner's office as soon as possible. There is no right of appeal to the Chief Coroner against the coroner's final decision.
16. When coroners request additional scientific examinations on specific organs or tissues to assist with establishing the cause of death or the identity of the person who has died, the appropriate next of kin will be informed. Again, if they have queries or concerns,

they should be directed to the coroner's office at the earliest opportunity, although the coroner's decision as to whether the examination should take place will be final.

17. In the unusual event of a second post-mortem being commissioned by coroners which is of the same type as one previously commissioned, and if family members are dissatisfied with a coroner's reason for commissioning such an examination, and they remain dissatisfied after discussion with the coroner's office, there will be a right of appeal to the Chief Coroner.
18. If the coroner decides *not* to hold a post-mortem, and family members wish to challenge the decision, they should discuss this with the coroner's office and, if they remain of the same view, they may appeal the decision to the Chief Coroner.
19. Family members will have a right, on request, to see reports of any post-mortems carried out although they should be aware they may find the details distressing.
20. These provisions may need to be varied in respect of post-mortems resulting from criminal or suspected criminal offences. The coroner's office or the Police Family Liaison Officer will discuss this with you in respect of those cases.

Keeping in touch

21. If the coroner continues his or her investigation following the post-mortem, the coroner's office will contact family members at least every three months to inform them of the status of the case, and explain any reasons for delays. This will not apply if family members have indicated that they only wish to be contacted when there is progress to report.

Inquests

22. When there is to be an inquest, information will be provided to family members of the timing, location, and the facilities available at its venue, wherever possible, at least four weeks before the start of the inquest.
23. Family members' views will be taken into account about the timing of the inquest and information will be provided to them by the coroner's office about, for example, the purpose of the inquest, who is likely to be present, and on the opportunities for participation in proceedings by addressing the coroner directly or through a legal representative. Information will also be provided about when legal aid may be available.
24. If the date and/or location of the inquest has to be changed, information will be provided, wherever possible, within five working days of the decision being taken.
25. Disclosure of all relevant documents to be used in an inquest will take place, on request, free of charge and in advance of an inquest, to those family members whom the coroner has determined have an interest in the investigation.
26. It is possible, for legal reasons, that not all documents that the coroner intends to use at an inquest will be able to be disclosed, or disclosed in full. On request, the coroner will explain the reasons why he or she has not disclosed a particular document, or part of a document.
27. Where the coroner decides to hold a pre-inquest hearing, those family members known to have an interest will be informed of the time, date and location, the purpose of the hearing and their rights and opportunities during it.
28. Wherever possible, an appropriate private room will be provided for bereaved relatives when they attend an inquest.
29. Some coroners now arrange for Court Support Services to operate on days when they hold inquests. The Support Service will welcome you when you arrive at the inquest, explain the process – working jointly with the coroner's office – and answer any queries you have before and immediately after the inquest. Where there is no Support Service, the coroner's office will fulfil this role.
30. With one or two exceptions, the media is free to report inquest proceedings, although there is a requirement under the Press Complaints Commission code of practice for

reporting to be sensitive and sympathetic to the feelings of the bereaved. The relevant section of the Press Complaints Commission code will be made available, on request, to family members.

31. If they are approached by the media, the coroner's office will not release anything other than outline details of specific current cases without the consent of the appropriate next of kin. Under no circumstances will photographs be released without the consent of the next of kin.

Reports to prevent future deaths

32. At the end of an inquest, the coroner will decide whether the evidence he or she has heard should lead to a report being made to an organisation which may have power to take action to prevent deaths in the future. The coroner will announce if he or she intends to make such a report.
33. Family members who the coroner has determined have an interest in the investigation will be sent a copy of the coroner's report, and any response, or a summary of the response, which an organisation makes.
34. The coroner will send a copy of the report made to the Chief Coroner who in turn will have a responsibility to provide a summary of reports made by all coroners, and the responses to them, to Parliament.

Other rights to participation

35. Family members will be informed by the coroner, after he or she has consulted with them, of any decision to refer a death for investigation by the coroner for a different area and the reasons for that decision. The same consultation will take place if the Chief Coroner directs that an investigation is carried out by a coroner for a different area. In that case, the responsibility for informing family members rests with the Chief Coroner.
36. Once a body is no longer required for the coroner's purposes, coroners will not, other than in exceptional circumstances, retain the body without the consent of the family. Exceptional circumstances may include when there is a dispute about whom the body should be released to. In cases where there is a criminal investigation as a result of the death, the requirement is that bodies will be released for funerals within a maximum of 30 days of the death, but normally it will be much sooner than this.
37. Sometimes, organs or tissues are retained for additional examination. In this instance, the coroner should reach advance agreement with the appropriate next of kin as to what should happen when they are no longer required for coroners' purposes. The coroner should convey the wishes of the next of kin to the relevant pathologist.

Review and appeal rights of coroners' judicial decisions

38. Family members who the coroner has designated as interested persons will have the right to appeal the following decisions:
    - if the coroner decides there will NOT be a post-mortem or that there will be a second post-mortem of the same type as previously requested
    - whether there will be an investigation by the coroner
    - whether to resume an investigation suspended by the coroner
    - whether an inquest should be held with a jury.
39. Additionally, the appropriate next of kin may make representations to the Chief Coroner if he or she is dissatisfied if, in exceptional circumstances, the coroner proposes to retain the body of the person who has died for more than 30 days after the death.
40. In most cases, if there is disagreement between the coroner and the family member about any of the above, it is likely to be resolved through discussion. If however, this is not possible, the family member can appeal to the Chief Coroner, setting out clearly

their grounds for appealing the decision, wherever possible within a maximum of 15 working days (within 1 working day if it concerns a post-mortem) of the decision being taken.

41. In addition, appeals will also be possible against decisions in relation to:
    - a coroner discontinuing an investigation before an inquest
    - the decision given at the end of an inquest.
42. The family will have 60 working days from the day the decision is taken to lodge their appeal in these instances, although consideration will be given as to whether appeals can be heard beyond this time limit.
43. Most appeals are likely to be decided on the papers. However, in any case where the Chief Coroner decides that an oral hearing is required, it is likely that additional time will be needed to give a judgment. The family will be kept informed by the Chief Coroner's office of the likely timescale.
44. The Chief Coroner's office will inform the person who has appealed (and others with an interest in the appeal) of the outcome of the appeal.

Deaths abroad

45. Coroners will investigate deaths abroad if the apparent circumstances of the death would have led them to have done so had the death occurred in England or Wales. The standards of service outlined in this charter, in particular (but not exclusively) in relation to post-mortems, may need to be varied because of the additional administrative difficulties in receiving information from overseas Governments.

Responsibilities of family members

46. Family members of the person who has died have a responsibility to provide all information to the coroner's office that is relevant to the investigation.
47. Family members, when requested, should treat with confidence any information or documents they have disclosed to them.
48. Family members should inform the coroner's office of any details, such as change of address, so they can be contacted promptly.
49. Family members should treat the coroner and his or her staff with courtesy and respect at all stages of the investigation.

Disability issues

50. Coroners will, as far as practicable and taking account of their statutory responsibilities, provide appropriate access to coroners' courts and offices. Reasonable adjustments will be made, wherever possible, to meet the needs of those with disabilities.

Availability of support and bereavement services

51. With the assistance of the Chief Coroner, coroners will maintain information on the main local and national voluntary bodies, support groups and faith groups which offer help or support to people who have been bereaved, including bereavement as a result of particular types of incidents or circumstances. They will make this information available to family members or their representatives unless they request otherwise.

Monitoring service standards

52. The Chief Coroner will require coroners to provide regular reports to him/her on their performance against national standards. The Chief Coroner will give the Lord Chancellor an annual report which will include an assessment of the consistency of standards between coroners' areas.
53. Independent inspections of the service will be carried out and will include consultation

with bereaved people. In addition, the Chief Coroner may arrange surveys of service users from time to time.

Other complaints and feedback

54. Bereaved people wishing to make a complaint about a failure to deliver other aspects of the service outlined in this charter should do so in the first instance to the coroner. If they are not satisfied with the response they should renew their complaint to the Chief Coroner. The Chief Coroner's address is: [TO BE INSERTED WHEN KNOWN]
55. Coroners are committed to providing a service which meets the needs of bereaved people at a sensitive time, and welcomes general feedback from bereaved people about their experiences, including feedback on where the service has performed well. They should be directed to the coroner who dealt with the case or the Chief Coroner.

Other responsibilities of the Chief Coroner

56. The Chief Coroner will be responsible for setting national minimum standards across a range of coroner functions. In terms of the services to bereaved families, this could include standards in relation to particular types of deaths or suspected deaths (for example – deaths on active military service, deaths as a result of atrocities or other disasters, deaths from particular illnesses such as mesothelioma, epilepsy or sudden adult death syndrome, and deaths apparently resulting from suicide). These are matters for the Chief Coroner to determine when he or she is appointed.
57. Similarly, this is a draft charter only, and is intended as a guide – to those with an interest – of the kinds of service it is envisaged will be provided in a reformed service.

INDEX